JESSICA
PRESCOTT

VEGAN GOODNESS
FEASTS

—

Plant-Based Meals
for Big & Little Gatherings

Hardie Grant

BOOKS

Contents

Dedication
*To Berlin, and all the people
who made our half-decade
there so special.*

There is nothing quite like sitting down to a meal with people you love...

For me, food has always been a way of connecting with people and nurturing my relationships. Growing up, no matter the state of our familial affairs, dinner was eaten around the kitchen table. The TV would be turned off and my dad would put on a record and we would eat, sometimes chatting, sometimes feuding, but always together.

My mum is an incredible cook and has worked in the bustling Hawke's Bay, New Zealand, food industry her entire life. She is renowned for putting on the best spreads and is always happy to cook whatever our hearts desire at Christmas time, instead of the usual Christmas fare. She embraced her role of cooking for a vegetarian teenager when I still lived at home and these days, we talk almost daily, swapping food stories, tips and ideas. As for her baking, it's the stuff of legend I tell you.

Sharing meals with loved ones is a ritual that followed me into adulthood, and now into parenthood, with my husband Andy and son, Louie, who was almost two at the time of writing this. There's something special about slowing down, sharing, and connecting with friends and family over food and conversation. Usually we come together for no reason other than to just be together, other times there's a celebration or commiseration at hand, but food – my most loyal and faithful friend – is always there.

Now that I am a mother and a member of an ever-growing extended family, I want to pass on the ritual of coming together over wholesome food to the little ones in my life. Louie and I already spend a lot of time in the kitchen together, and I hope that it will be as happy a place for the next generation as it is for me; that they will always find comfort and nourishment in my pantry and at my table; and that my nieces, nephews and fairy godchildren will always cherish the memories of the epic birthday cakes I made for them.

Kiwis are known for their insatiable wanderlust and I am no exception. In 2012, I moved to Berlin with my then-boyfriend and now-husband, Andy. What was supposed to be a year-long 'working holiday' ended up being a five-year love affair with the cold, rude, dirty, but wonderful, city of Berlin.

Once upon a time, during our early Berlin years, dinner parties were rowdy, all-night affairs – the kind where every guest brings a bottle of wine and every drop gets drunk. After becoming parents, dinners became more intimate and often took place before friends ventured off into the Berlin night. I loved that even though we were constantly growing and changing, we still had dinner... we will always have dinner.

My little family lives in Melbourne now, but our Berlin apartment had a special kind of magic. Even in its most chaotic state, it was a place of connection and creativity. My son, my first book, *Vegan Goodness*, and most of this book you now hold in your hands were all born there. As an ode to its magic, and as a way of remembering what was, I wanted to share some of the creations that have made it from my Berlin kitchen to the bellies of my loved ones, as well as some of the creations that have made it from their kitchens to mine, over the past five years.

There's a feeling about feasting and food preparation that I just love. I've said it before and I'll probably say it a thousand times more over the course of my life, but my kitchen really is my happy place. Sometimes I don't have the capacity for more than a smoothie and a piece of toast, but – when occasion calls – nothing beats spending all day and night cooking, with Louie asleep or playing happily alongside me, and Andy on hand to help with the inevitable mountain of dishes.

I also find there is something incredibly romantic about cooking together. Perhaps it's because it only happens on special occasions – holidays spent with family, weekends away with your best friends – but, to me, sitting around a large wooden table with a bottle of wine and a bunch of loved ones, chatting while we peel and chop and prep the ingredients for a meal we are going to enjoy together, is quite unbeatable.

I've written this book so that you can follow the recipes I've suggested, or pluck out components that you like the sound of, to create your own feast. Whether you're in a cooking mood and want to spend a day in the kitchen, or going to a potluck with a bunch of friends and a medley of assorted dishes. Or perhaps you just want a simple feast, to share with your housemates, your lover or your child. No matter your situation, there is something in this book for you. New things. Naughty things. Delicious things. Vegan things.

About the portion sizes

In these recipes a range is given, such as 'Serves 4–8': meaning it will feed 4 if served as a main dish, 8 if served with an array of other things, such as in a potluck, buffet or multi-course meal. It's always difficult to give exact numbers, as it depends on personal preference (my friends are enthusiastic eaters), and whether or not there are toddlers or teenagers involved, so use this as a guide and remember: this book is about feasting and leftovers are the best.

Since making the decision to be *as vegan as possible* at the beginning of 2013, my passion for sharing food has deepened, because I am endlessly inspired and excited by vegan creations. The things you can do with vegetables really is endless.

These days, almost everyone has a friend or family member who chooses not to eat animal products. Ever since the World Health Organisation declared processed meat products to be carcinogenic, I get almost daily messages – sometimes from an old school friend, other times from a complete stranger – telling me they are going vegan, that their formerly meat-loving families are requesting vegan and vegetarian meals, or that they are feeling the desire to eat more plant-based meals. This is born both out of curiosity and out of mindfulness, and coming with it is the realisation that vegan food isn't just for vegans. The new wave of TV series and films and documentaries such as 'What the Health', 'Dominion', 'Food Matters' and 'Okja' have also played a significant role in helping people redefine what healthy, ethical and environmentally friendly eating really is.

I'm not here to try and convince you to go vegan, you'll figure out what works best for you in your own time, and that's likely to be fluid and ever-changing. All I want is to inspire a shift, that sees meals without meat and dairy just as commonplace as (if not more common than) meals *with* them. This is the change I wish to see, a change that is vital for the wellbeing of our beautiful planet and everyone who is lucky enough to inhabit her.

My first book, *Vegan Goodness*, was almost a vegan cooking 101. Simple, inexpensive recipes, most of them a vegan-ised version of things that people were already familiar with. This book is a little more complex. The recipes are still very achievable for a confident and passionate home cook, but some of them might be a bit overwhelming for beginner cooks, who might not have as many of the ingredients on hand as someone who likes to cook frequently and with wholefoods. The good thing is that even a beginner cook can make a salad or smash some potatoes, so I hope that no matter what stage you are at in your cooking journey, you will find recipes in here that will inspire and excite you.

Share your creations with me on social media by tagging Wholy Goodness and using the hashtag **#VGFeasts**.

**New things.
Naughty things.
Delicious things.
Vegan things.**

Guten Appetit!
xx

♡ Jess
xx.

Kitchen & Pantry Staples

Herbs – I always have basil, parsley and coriander (cilantro) on hand, and buy rosemary, thyme, and so on, as required

Greens – baby spinach, rocket (arugula), broccoli, kale, fresh peas, beans or Brussels sprouts

A few salady things – avocados, tomatoes, cucumber and carrots

Quick-cook veggies – aubergines (eggplants), courgettes (zucchini) and mushrooms

Starchy rooty veg – potatoes, sweet potatoes and pumpkin (squash)

Flavour-makers – red onions, brown onions, garlic and lemons

Bananas – if you love smoothies, get into the habit of always buying them to have on hand

Seasonal fruits – for me it's pomegranates, berries, figs, pears and stone fruits

REFRIGERATOR AND FREEZER
Tofu
Frozen peas
Puff pastry

Grains – wholegrain rice, quinoa, wholewheat couscous, freekeh, barley, oats. Also an assortment of puffed grains such as quinoa, amaranth and rice

Pasta – wholegrain pasta, spelt pasta and chickpea- flour pasta (available from health food stores)

Legumes – chickpeas (garbanzo beans), black beans, white beans, green lentils, beluga lentils, red lentils, split peas, black-eyed peas

Nuts – almonds (whole, flaked and slivered), cashews, walnuts, hazelnuts, pine nuts

Seeds – sesame, sunflower, hemp, pumpkin, chia, flax

Dried fruit – dates (both Medjool and Deglet Noor), figs, apricots, goji berries, dehydrated raspberries, cranberries

Flours – wheat, wholewheat, spelt, wholemeal spelt, rice, buckwheat, coconut, almond, hazelnut, tapioca (arrowroot) and my most-beloved chickpea flour (sometimes called besan or gram flour)

Sugar – coconut, rapadura, demerera and raw cane

Cocoa powder, **cacao nibs** and **chocolate chips**

Psyllium husk

Coconut – desiccated, shredded and flaked

Baking powder and **bicarbonate of soda** (baking soda)

TINNED
Pulses – chickpeas (garbanzo beans), black beans, white beans, lentils

Vegetables – tomatoes, jackfruit
Coconut milk

CONDIMENTS
Sweeteners – maple syrup, date syrup, rice malt syrup, barley syrup
Nut butters – almond, hazelnut, smooth and crunchy peanut butter, hulled and unhulled tahini
Vinegars – balsamic, apple cider, white and red wine vinegars
Ferments – kimchi, sauerkraut
Pickled onions, **pickled gherkins**
Antipasti – olives, capers, sun-dried tomatoes
Mustard
Tamari or **soy sauce**
Nutritional yeast flakes
Sea salt and black salt
Miso paste
Liquid smoke
Some kind of fancy fermented **cashew cheese** (this is only since living in Melbourne where nut-based cheeses are off the hook!)

OILS
Olive oil, for salad dressings, pasta sauces and so on
Coconut oil, for baking
Sesame oil, for Asian foods
Avocado oil, for high-heat cooking

SPICES AND DRIED HERBS
basil, bay leaves, black peppercorns, cardamom, chilli flakes, cinnamon, coriander, cumin, curry powder, fenugreek, garam masala, lovage, nutmeg, oregano, paprika (sweet and smoked), parsley, sage, sumac, thyme, turmeric

SOME EXTRA NOTES ON INGREDIENTS IN THIS BOOK

Aquafaba The vegan egg replacement that has revolutionised vegan baking. From *aqua*, meaning water, and *faba*, meaning bean – more specifically, the water from tinned chickpeas (garbanzo beans).

Black salt AKA *kala namak*. I heard about this for years before I finally found some in Berlin's vegan supermarket. True to what I'd heard, it is the absolute bomb. Hailed by Ayurvedic practitioners for its medicinal qualities, it contains sulphur, which lends an eggy flavour to tofu and chickpea dishes, and adds authentic depth to Indian cooking.

Cashews If using a high-speed food processor/blender you don't need to bother with soaking them and, in fact, if you live somewhere with hard water, soaking them may be counterproductive. Instead, boil them in water for 15 minutes, then drain and rinse, and proceed with the recipe.

Chickpea flour AKA gram or besan flour. Since writing my first book, I've developed a full-blown obsession with the stuff. It started by trying to bulk up the nutrition in the food I make for Louie and, as I experimented with it and got to know this flour, I realised the numerous ways I can use it. If you

don't already have some, grab some next time you see it at the supermarket, as many of the recipes in this book call for it – you are bound to need it shortly!

Coconut oil I bake with coconut oil, but canola oil, rice bran oil and olive oil are all okay alternatives. You can also use a blend of all, if you prefer.

Curry powder This is easy to find – make sure you buy one that contains fenugreek, as this adds a sweetness that makes it insanely delicious.

Dates I use Medjool dates for most of my baking recipes, because they are so big and soft and easy to work with. I've noticed that in some parts of the world they are stored in the refrigerator, however I find them much easier to work with when they are stored at room temperature. If you prefer to store yours in the fridge, just get them out a few hours before cooking. A cheaper alternative – and what I used to buy a lot in Berlin – are the boxes of soft dates that you find at Middle Eastern stores. They are smaller than Medjool, so you need to use two of them for every individual Medjool.

Milk Most of the plant-based milks are interchangeable in the recipes, depending on what you have in. However, for baking, the only milk I would avoid using is rice milk (it's too thin and overly sweet for baked goods).

Salt I am a salt junkie and have a kazillion different types on my spice shelf, but for cooking I always use fine sea salt. If you have flakes, grind them first to get the right amount, as 1 tsp fine sea salt is a lot saltier than 1 tsp flaked sea salt.

Tofu There was no tofu in my first book but, since doing more homework and learning how to make it myself, I have come to realise that it's actually not bad for you and when you do it right, it's really, really delicious. The tofu I use in this book is firm tofu. Drain and press it first to get all the excess moisture out, which allows the tofu to soak up all the yummy flavours you are adding to it. To do this, simply remove it from its packet and pour all the excess liquid down the drain. If it's a thick block, cut it in half through the middle. Wrap the tofu in a clean tea towel and place it under something heavy (a large wooden board with a cast iron pot is my favourite weight, but cookbooks work well too!) for at least half an hour.

Vanilla I prefer bourbon vanilla powder, but that is not always an affordable option. Next best is vanilla extract, then essence and finally vanilla aroma. The latter is not good quality at all, but I have to admit that, if you get the right brand, it can be delicious. Just use whatever you have on hand or whatever is affordable when you buy your groceries.

Grain & Legume Cooking Times and Techniques

GRAINS

One thing I find to be consistent amongst grains and the multitude of other things parading as grains (hello quinoa, buckwheat and couscous), is that not many people know exactly how to cook them. I see all kinds of techniques in the kitchens of my loved ones, most of them confessing that that have no idea what they are doing as they fuss over a pot of sludgy grains and too much water. Their methods invariably work, but seem to cause more stress than necessary. There is an easy way to get perfect grains every time with minimal effort. Here's how:

First, rinse the grains in a fine-meshed sieve until the water runs clear. This will remove any residue and, in the case of grains such as quinoa, it will also remove the bitterness.

Place the grains in a saucepan with the specified amount of water and 1 teaspoon sea salt (see chart below). Stir once, then cover with a lid and bring to the boil. **Do not remove the lid or stir again.** Once boiling, lower to a simmer and allow to cook for the specified amount of time. Once cooked, remove from the heat and allow to sit in the pan for another 5–10 minutes, before removing the lid and fluffing the grains with a fork. You can add a little olive oil at this stage too, if you like.

If you forget to set a timer or if you are unsure whether all the water has been absorbed, use a spoon to pull back some of the grains and check if there is still water in the bottom of the pan. Whatever you do, don't stir the grains to see if there is still water in the pot.

Note: Compare any two cookbooks and the recommended water requirement / cooking times / final yield will always be different. This is because the older the grains, the drier they are, and the longer they will take to cook. Variables such as your water quality, stovetop force and pans also play a role in determining your final cooking time.

* A pasta, not a grain, but great when you need something quick

Grain (1 cup)	Water (per 1 cup grain)	Cooking Time	Yield
Amaranth	2 cups (firm grains) 3 cups (porridge-y grains)	20 minutes	2 cups
Barley	3 cups	1 hour	4 cups
Black Rice	2 cups	40 minutes	3 cups
Brown Rice	2 cups	30–50 minutes	3 cups
Buckwheat	2 cups	10–20 minutes	3½ cups
Bulgur	1½ cups	10–15 minutes	3 cups
Wholewheat Couscous*	1½ cups	Pour over boiling water and cover with a tea towel for 5 minutes	3 cups
Farro	3 cups	20–25 minutes	3 cups
Cracked Freekeh	3 cups	15–20 minutes	
Whole Freekeh	4 cups	30–40 minutes	3 cups
Millet	2 cups	25 minutes	4 cups
Quinoa	2 cups	15 minutes	3 cups
Red Rice	2 cups	45 minutes	3 cups
Spelt	4 cups	1 hour	3 cups

LEGUMES

Filled with fibre, protein and antioxidants, legumes are an incredibly important part of the vegan diet. Any non-vegan dish can have its meat substituted for a legume of some kind, such as chickpeas (garbanzo beans) instead of chicken in a Thai curry, or lentils instead of minced (ground) meat in a Bolognese. You can turn any bean into a tasty dip with the addition of garlic, salt, lemon, cumin and tahini, and you can use them in sweet treats too.

My favourite legumes to cook with are black beans, chickpeas, white beans and lentils, so I always have both tinned and dried on hand. Split peas are also good to have around to throw into soups.

Tinned beans are a godsend in a pinch, but if you get into the habit of cooking a bag of dried beans every week, you can use some in a meal, pop some in the refrigerator for salads throughout the week, and freeze what you don't think you'll use.

About soaking

Lentils and split peas are fast-cooking and do not require any pre-soaking to get them to cook, however soaking will break down the phytic acid in them, enabling you to better absorb their iron. Beans and chickpeas take a little longer to cook, so it is customary to soak them overnight, which reduces both their cooking time and their gas-inducing sugars, as well as breaking down the aforementioned phytic acid. The exception to this is black beans. I rarely soak them because doing so reduces their flavour significantly. I get that not everyone has time to cook their black beans from scratch though, so I've included recipes that utilize both methods in this book.

To prep: Always check over your beans or lentils before rinsing to make sure no tiny little sticks or stones are hiding in there. I find a fine-mesh sieve to be perfect for this step. It's rare you will find one, but worth the effort to prevent any damage to your mouth. Rinse with cold water to remove any residue.

To soak: Pop the beans or lentils into a large saucepan or bowl and fill with warm water, so they are covered by at least 5 cm (2 in). Cover and leave for 8–16 hours. Drain off the soaking liquid and fill the pan with fresh water before cooking.

You can also 'quick-soak' beans: put them in a saucepan, cover with 5 cm (2 in) water, bring to the boil and then turn the heat off and allow to sit with the lid on for 1 hour.

To cook lentils and split peas

Place in a saucepan, cover with at least 5 cm (2 in) water, add a teaspoon of salt, bring to the boil, then simmer for 10–30 minutes (refer to the chart for more detailed cooking times). You can also put them directly into soups, stews, etc. Be aware that they will soak up some of the cooking liquid, so keep an eye on the pot and add more water as necessary.

To cook beans

Bring to the boil, and then lower to a simmer so that the beans remain intact. Add a teaspoon of salt and if you are turning them into something mushy, add 1 teaspoon bicarbonate of soda (baking soda) to help them along the way. Allow to bubble away for 1–2 hours. The chart to the left will help, but final cooking time will depend on the age of your beans – the older they are, the drier they are and the more water and time they will need. I usually pop them on while I am pottering around the house, adding water and checking them regularly. I know they are ready once I can squish them on the side of the pot with the back of a spoon.

Legume (1 cup)	Cooking Time		Yield
	Soaked	*Unsoaked*	
Adzuki Beans	45 minutes–1 hour	1–2 hours	3½ cups
Black Beans	45 minutes–1 hour	1–2 hours	3½ cups
Black-Eyed Peas	45 minutes–1 hour	1–2 hours	3 cups
Cannellini (White Beans)	45 minutes–1 hour	1–3 hours	3 cups
Chickpeas (Garbanzo Beans)	45 minutes–1 hour	2–3 hours	3 cups
Fava Beans	45 minutes–1 hour	1–3 hours	2½ cups
Kidney Beans	1–1½ hours	2–3 hours	3 cups
Lentils (Brown or Green)	15–20 minutes	30 minutes	3½ cups
Lentils (Puy or Beluga)	10–15 minutes	20 minutes	3 cups
Lentils (Red)	10–15 minutes	15–20 minutes	3 cups
Mung Beans	45 minutes–1 hour	1–3 hours	3 cups
Navy Beans	45 minutes–1 hour	1–3 hours	2½ cups
Pinto Beans	45 minutes–1 hour	1–3 hours	3 cups
Split Peas	10–30 minutes	1 hour	2½ cups
Soy Beans	2¼ hours	2–3 hours	3 cups

Brunches & Pit Stops

After having my son Louie, life suddenly became very, very busy and we had to be creative with how we caught up with friends. Day hangs make so much more sense for parents who are woken early by their kids and are exhausted by the time childless folk eat dinner. Enter brunches, morning teas, smoothie dates and afternoon playdates - more occasions to come together over food.

The food in this chapter is perfect for casual daytime feasting. Most of it can be served buffet-style, which is ideal for families who all like their first meal of the day at different times. It allows you to eat while chasing little ones around and, of course, it allows for a variety of taste buds and appetites.

Muffins for Everyone

*Makes
12 small or
6 large*

A staple of my childhood, muffins have been my friends for as long as I can remember. Here, I share three of my favourite recipes: Decadent Berry & Dark Chocolate Muffins, for when you need a treat; Health Bomb Carrot & Apple Muffins, a recipe I developed with little ones in mind; and Banana Walnut Muffins, which I have been making since time immemorial. All follow the same easy method that my mum taught me when I was a kid, and they are easy to transport, making them perfect for lakeside picnics and afternoon playdates alike.

Preheat the oven to 180°C (350°F/Gas 4). Either grease a muffin tin (pan) or line the cups with paper muffin cups or baking paper.

Combine all the wet ingredients in a large mixing bowl and set aside. Sift all the dry ingredients into a separate large mixing bowl. Add the chunky ingredients and roughly combine. Make a well in the centre of the mixture and pour in the wet ingredients, stirring until just combined. This is a trick my mum taught me when I was a child – you don't want to over-mix the ingredients or the muffins will be tough instead of fluffy. Spoon the mixture into the muffin cups and sprinkle with the toppings.

Bake in the hot oven for the designated cooking time (see below). Check that they are cooked by inserting a toothpick into the centre of a muffin – if some batter sticks to it, pop them back in the oven for another 2–5 minutes.

Baking times:

Decadent Berry & Dark Chocolate:
30 minutes for small / 40 minutes for large

Health Bomb Carrot & Apple:
20 minutes for small / 30 minutes for large

Banana Walnut:
20 minutes for small / 30 minutes for large

Decadent Berry & Dark Chocolate

Shopping list
Wet ingredients:
250 ml (8½ fl oz/1 cup) soy milk
    (or any other plant-based milk,
    except rice milk)
1 teaspoon apple cider vinegar
1 teaspoon pure vanilla extract
2 tablespoons chia seeds
3 tablespoons melted coconut oil
    or olive oil

Dry ingredients:
125 g (4 oz/1 cup) spelt flour
60 g (2 oz/½ cup) millet flour
100 g (3½ oz/½ cup) sugar (any kind)
1 teaspoon baking powder
1 teaspoon bicarbonate of soda
    (baking soda)
pinch of salt

Chunky ingredients:
200 g (7 oz) frozen mixed berries
    (preferably no strawberries as they
    are too large and will make the
    muffins a bit soggy)
100 g (3½ oz) vegan dark
    chocolate, broken into chunks

Topping:
extra dark chocolate, to sprinkle
3 tablespoons puffed quinoa

Health Bomb Carrot & Apple

Shopping list
Wet ingredients:
250 ml (8½ fl oz/1 cup) soy milk
    (or any other plant-based milk,
    except rice milk)
1 teaspoon apple cider vinegar
1 teaspoon pure vanilla extract
3 tablespoons melted coconut oil
    or olive oil
1 ripe and spotty banana, mashed
    until smooth
150 g (5 oz/1 cup) grated (shredded)
    apple
135 g (4 oz/1 cup) grated (shredded)
    carrot
1 tablespoon maple or date syrup
    (optional)

Dry ingredients:
185 g (6½ oz/1½ cup) spelt flour
50 g (1¾ oz/½ cup) almond flour
¾ teaspoon bicarbonate of soda
    (baking soda)
¾ teaspoon baking powder
1 teaspoon ground cinnamon
pinch of salt

Chunky ingredients:
70 g (2½ oz/½ cup) raisins

Topping:
3 tablespoons oats

Banana Walnut

Shopping list
Wet ingredients:
4 ripe and spotty bananas, mashed
    until smooth
80 ml (2½ fl oz/⅓ cup) oil (coconut,
    olive and rice bran all work well)
35 g (1¼oz/⅓ cup) sugar (any kind: rice
    malt syrup or maple syrup will work too)
1 teaspoon vanilla extract

Dry ingredients:
200 g (7 oz/1½ cups) flour (wholemeal
    spelt, white all-purpose or a blend
    of spelt, buckwheat, etc.)
1 teaspoon bicarbonate of soda
    (baking soda)
pinch of salt

Chunky ingredients:
large handful of walnuts (about 50 g/2 oz),
    finely chopped
large handful of vegan chocolate chips
    (about 50 g/2 oz) (if you're feeling
    naughty)

Topping:
additional walnuts (optional)

Health Bomb
Carrot &
AppleMuffins
(page 15)

Smoothies

Enjoying a smoothie together is a great way of pausing and nourishing yourselves, be it at the beginning, middle or end of the day. Their role can be that of a snack, meal, side dish or dessert and, to little ones, a smoothie and a muffin makes for a perfect, energy-intensive, high-fibre meal.

Place all the ingredients in a blender and blend until smooth. Enjoy immediately or pop it in the refrigerator for up to a day. It may separate a little but give it a shake or a stir and it's good as new.

All serve 2-4

Banoffee Smoothie

If you've never tried coffee and banana before, your reaction right now is probably the same as my own when my beloved friend Shan first shared the idea with me, way back in 2013. It was something she'd stumbled upon and swiftly fallen in love with during her travels through Mexico. Open-minded as I am when it comes to food, I just couldn't believe it would be good. Oh, how wrong I was. This was at the height of my affair with hazelnut milk, so I have written the recipe to follow suit, though it can be made with any plant-based milk you prefer. It's. So. Damn. Good.

Shopping list
2 ripe and spotty bananas, preferably frozen
2 Medjool dates
200 ml (7 fl oz/generous ¾ cup) espresso (or thereabouts)
500 ml (17 fl oz/2 cups) unsweetened plant-based milk

4pm Choc Attack

This is for when those afternoon chocolate cravings strike, but you are *trying* to be healthy. This smoothie is perfect for pregnant and lactating mothers, who can easily devour a block of chocolate in one sitting.

Shopping list
2 ripe and spotty bananas
2 Medjool dates
2 tablespoons shredded coconut
2 tablespoons raw cashews
2 tablespoons cacao nibs
  (roasted if possible)
1 tablespoon peanut butter
500 ml (17 fl oz/2 cups) water
pinch of bourbon vanilla powder
  or a drop of vanilla extract

Louie's Green Smoothie

I make this for Louie every day. At the time of writing, he is not the most adventurous of eaters, which means getting a smoothie into him gives me much relief. Sometimes I make a large one if he is sharing it with me or with his little buddies, but if I am making it just for him, I use half a banana and scale the rest of the recipe accordingly.

Shopping list
2 ripe and spotty bananas
2 Medjool dates
2 large handfuls of baby spinach
1 tablespoon peanut or almond butter
small handful of cashews
500 ml (17 fl oz/2 cups) water
pinch of bourbon vanilla powder
  or a drop of vanilla extract
optional extras: hemp seeds or
  lucuma powder

Blueberry Bomb

This one is a classic that I come back to time and time again because it never fails to hit the spot.

Shopping list
2 ripe and spotty bananas
125 g (4 oz/1 cup) blueberries
1 Medjool date
2 tablespoons almond butter
1 tablespoon hemp seeds
500 ml (17 fl oz/2 cups) plant-based milk
  of your choice
optional extras: handful of spinach

Baked Coconut-Milk French Toast

This ever-versatile crowd pleaser is one of the most popular recipes on my blog, and for good reason – it's delicious, easy to make and can be topped with whatever fruits are in season. Where the version on my blog is cooked in a frying pan (skillet), this version is baked, leaving your hands free for other important hosting tasks, such as making drinks and greeting your loved ones. It can be prepared ahead and reheated when it's time to eat, making it perfect for a weekend or holiday-season brunch party.

Preheat the oven to 180°C (350°F/Gas 4).

Put the coconut milk, bananas, cinnamon and nutmeg into a blender or food processor and blend into a smooth batter. Pour half of the batter into a shallow baking dish that's just large enough to fit all the slices of bread, then place the bread in the dish. Don't be afraid to squish the slices a little to fit them all in, the odd shapes add character. Pour the remaining batter over the bread slices and then jiggle the slices around until they are all nicely coated in the batter.

Pop the whole thing in the hot oven and cook for 1 hour, flipping the bread slices about halfway through the cooking time.

To serve, I've stacked slices of French toast with coconut yoghurt and fresh berries between the layers, plopped a generous spoonful of almond butter on top, put blueberry poached pears on the side, before drenching the entire thing with maple syrup. When enjoying with loved ones, I suggest serving the French toast and all the toppings buffet-style and allowing everyone to decorate their toast themselves.

Note: It's important that you should use real maple syrup, not maple *flavoured* syrup, which is terrible tasting and terrible for you! If you can't find the real thing or it is a bit pricey where you live, date syrup is a delicious and healthy alternative.

Serves 4 and can easily be doubled if feeding 6–8

Shopping list
For the French toast:
400 ml (13 fl oz) tin coconut milk
2 ripe and spotty bananas
½ teaspoon ground cinnamon
¼ teaspoon ground nutmeg
8 thick slices soft white bread,
   cut in half if they are very wide

To serve:
coconut yoghurt
fresh berries
almond butter
Blueberry Poached Pears (page 22)
maple syrup (see Note)
or whatever you wish:
   figs, poached apples, stone
   fruits and bananas also make
   delicious toppings

Blueberry Poached Pears

The humble pear is a beautiful fruit in its own right. Poach it with blueberries and it looks like something from another galaxy. Andy likes to call these 'nebula pears'.

Place the whole pears in a small or medium-sized saucepan (you want them to be a little bit cramped). Add the blueberries and pour in enough water to just cover (about 1 litre/35 fl oz/4 cups). It's okay if the fruit is bobbing out of the water a tiny bit, you can turn it as it cooks. Place on a medium heat and bring to the boil, then lower to a simmer and cook for 20 minutes.

Leave to cool in the water, then remove and slice down the middle. Serve with the French toast (as pictured on page 20), pancakes, waffles, porridge (oatmeal), muesli, granola, yoghurt, custard, chocolate, caramel… The uses are endless, really!

Note: Don't discard the water. Pop it in the refrigerator and use it the following day to give your porridge, smoothies or pancakes a bright purple hue!

Serves 4–8

Shopping list
4–6 pears, peeled
125 g (4 oz/1 cup)
 frozen blueberries

Easy Fruit Galette

Galettes are so easy to make, yet their freeform, rustic charm never fails to elicit the most joyous reactions from my loved ones. Even my toast-loving husband will gladly devour this as his first meal of the day. This recipe uses sweet late-summer nectarines and blackberries but you can use whatever fruit is in season, be it other stone fruits in the summer months or pears and apples in the cooler months.

Preheat the oven to 180°C (350°F/Gas 4).

For the pastry: Place the flour, oats, coconut oil and maple syrup in a large mixing bowl and mix with a fork until the ingredients are combined but the mixture is still crumbly. Add 3-5 tablespoons water, 1 tablespoon at a time, stirring between additions, until the mixture sticks together. (How much water is required will vary, not only from cook to cook, but from day to day, depending on the humidity.) Lightly knead into a ball in the bowl and then turn out onto a floured surface. Press into a circle with your fingertips, then flip and roll out with a lightly floured rolling pin. Continue to flip and roll, dusting the top with a little flour each time, until your pastry dough is a 30-40 cm (12-16 in) circle. If you are having difficulty rolling, let the dough rest for a moment while you prepare the fruit.

Once the pastry is fully rolled, carefully transfer it to a large baking tray (sheet). It will hang over the edges but that's fine, as the overhang will soon be folded over the fruit filling.

For the filling: Cut each nectarine into 8-12 wedges. If the fruit is not yet ripe enough to remove from the stone, cut around the stone and then cut these pieces into thinner slices. Place them in a large mixing bowl, along with the coconut sugar and cinnamon. Toss to coat and then pile into the centre of the pastry. Spread the pieces out, leaving a clear border of 5-10 cm (2-4 in), then pile the blackberries on top.

Fold up the edges of the pastry to partially cover the fruit, pinching the corners together to help them stay in place. Brush the pastry with milk of choice and then bake the galette in the hot oven for 30-40 minutes, until the pastry is golden brown and the fruit soft and gooey.

Allow to cool for 10 minutes, then serve, topped with coconut yoghurt, chopped pistachios and a glass of something yummy. That's how to be fancy with minimal effort.

Serves 4-8

Shopping list
For the pastry:
125 g (4 oz/1 cup) spelt flour, plus extra for dusting
50 g (2 oz/½ cup) instant oats
80 ml (2½ fl oz/⅓ cup) coconut oil
1 tablespoon maple syrup

For the filling:
5-6 nectarines
2 teaspoons coconut sugar
½ teaspoon ground cinnamon
1-2 large handfuls of blackberries (about 150 g/5 oz)

plant-based milk of choice, for brushing

To serve:
coconut yoghurt
chopped pistachios

There are two things that make a bagel a bagel, other than its shape. One is the slow rise – letting your dough prove in the fridge overnight. The other is the rapid boil – boiling them in sweetened water before baking them in a hot oven. Without these two steps, a bagel is just a piece of bread with a hole in the middle, which is what you will find at most supermarkets. Lucky for us, Laurel from Fine Bagels in Berlin (*the* Berlin bagel supplier) has shared her foolproof recipe with me, so that you can enjoy legit, New-York-style bagels, any time you like, even if you don't live near a reputable bagel supplier.

Fine Bagels

Make these in the evening and bake in the morning, before brunch.

There's nothing better than biting into a freshly cooked bagel that's still warm from the oven and piled high with your favourite toppings. When I photographed this recipe, chanterelles were in season and I couldn't resist piling them onto the fresh bagels with vegan ricotta, chives and rocket (arugula). My friends devoured them with gusto.

For family get-togethers, we pop fresh bagels on the table with favourite toppings on the side so that everyone can enjoy them whichever way they like, whenever they like. We always have avocado, cream cheese, hummus, tomato, cucumber and a leafy green of some kind. Vegan ricotta, or mushrooms cooked in a little bit of olive oil, lemon juice, salt and parsley, are also a treat, as is Scrambled Tofu (see page 28), sprouts, nut butter, coconut bacon (there's a recipe in my first book and on my blog for that), tempeh, smoked tofu, and so on.

In a large mixing bowl, whisk together the flour, salt and yeast so that they are evenly distributed. Add the barley malt syrup and water, mixing to incorporate, then begin kneading. If you have a stand mixer with a dough hook, let 'er rip for 4–5 minutes, but if you're kneading by hand, this is the hard part – 6 minutes hand kneading. Bagel dough should be tough. Still, you don't want any dry bits, so add a little bit more water if it needs it.

Once the dough is kneaded (it should be smooth and NOT sticky), place the ball of dough into a lightly oiled bowl. Cover with a damp tea towel or cling film (plastic wrap) and place in the refrigerator for 1 hour.

After this time, the dough should be soft and easier to work with, and should have risen by about 25 per cent. Remove from the bowl and gently form into a log shape, being careful not to knock out all the air. Cut into 12 even pieces, press into rough balls, and let rest for another 5 minutes, to relax the gluten. Roll each piece into a log about 3 cm (1 in) in diameter. Give each a twist and attach one end to the other with a strong pinch. The twist helps maintain the shape of the bagel during proving and the pinch stops it from falling apart during the boiling stage.

Place your bagels on a baking tray (sheet) lined with baking parchment and cover with cling film. Chill in the refrigerator for 12–18 hours, with the refrigerator set to its coldest setting.

The next day, preheat the oven to 200°C (400°F/Gas 6). Bring a large pan of water to the boil, adding salt and barley malt syrup to taste. Drop in a few bagels at a time. They should sink and then float to the top. Boil for 1 minute. Remove from the water with tongs and place on a baking tray lined with baking parchment. Sprinkle with sesame seeds, poppy seeds, or whatever you like! Transfer the bagels to the hot oven and bake for about 12 minutes, until they are a rich golden brown. Devour!

Makes 12 bagels

Shopping list
1 kg (2 lb 3 oz) bread flour
24 g (4¼ teaspoons) sea salt
12 g (4 teaspoons) instant yeast
 (dry active)
2 tablespoons barley malt syrup,
 plus additional barley malt syrup
 to season cooking water
500 ml (17 fl oz/2 cups)
 room-temperature water
oil, for greasing
additional salt to season
 cooking water
sesame seeds, poppy seeds,
 or whatever you'd like to
 sprinkle on top

Scrambled Tofu & Green Pea Wraps

Scrambled tofu is often served as an alternative to scrambled eggs, but it's an incredibly delicious dish in its own right. This version is served with crispy potatoes, green peas, avo and herbs and wrapped up in a lightly toasted tortilla, making for a wholesome and moreish savoury brunch dish.

Preheat the oven to 180°C (350°F/Gas 4).

Remove the peas from the freezer, cover with warm water and set aside. Combine the seasoning spices and nutritional yeast in a small bowl or cup and set aside.

Heat 2 tablespoons of the oil in a large frying pan (skillet) over a medium-high heat. Add the potatoes and sprinkle with salt. Cook for 5-10 minutes, stirring frequently, until golden brown and easily pierced with the tip of a knife. Transfer to an oven tray or dish and place in the oven to keep warm.

Add the remaining 1 tablespoon oil to the same pan and crumble in the tofu. Sprinkle the spice mixture over the top and, using a spatula, stir until all the tofu is nicely coated in the spice mixture - it should be bright yellow. Drain the peas and add these to the scramble, along with a splash of water if the tofu is starting to stick to the pan. Cook, stirring frequently, until parts of the tofu start to turn golden, about 10 minutes.

Pop your wraps in the oven to heat through slightly and then transfer them to a plate and top with fillings. I like to go potatoes, scramble, avocado, creamy thing, green things, lime, but you can build them in whichever way you like and, of course, adjust the toppings to suit. Pickled onions, jalapeños, lettuce, baby spinach or kale also make great additions.

Enjoy immediately, with coffee or an espresso martini, or both.

Note: Bulk this up by serving with the black beans from page 64. You can purée them or keep them whole - they compliment these breakfast wraps perfectly.

Serves 4-8

Shopping list
125 g (4 oz/1 cup) frozen peas
3 tablespoons olive oil
350-400 g (12-14 oz) baby
  potatoes, cut into 1 cm
  (½ in) cubes
400 g (14 oz) firm tofu, drained
  and lightly pressed
8 x 20 cm (8 in) wheat tortilla wraps
1 large or 2 small avocados, sliced
salt to taste

**For the tofu scramble
  seasoning:**
½ teaspoon turmeric
½ teaspoon black salt
½ teaspoon onion powder
½ teaspoon garlic powder
½ teaspoon ground coriander
2 tablespoons nutritional yeast
  (yeast flakes)

To garnish:
soy yoghurt, sour cream
  or cashew cream
fresh coriander (cilantro) leaves
microherbs
fresh lime, to squeeze

Wild Mushroom & Kale Quiche

Delicious hot or cold and easy to transport, this quiche is a great dish to have in your repertoire. It works as a stand alone brunch dish, or can be taken to a potluck or picnic and enjoyed with an array of other yummy things.

Preheat the oven to 180°C (350°F/Gas 4). Grease a 20 x 30 cm (8 x 12 in) or 26 cm (10 in) round pie dish with a generous amount of coconut oil or margarine.

For the pastry crust: Place the flour and salt in a large mixing bowl. Work in the coconut oil or margarine with your fingers and then add the water, little by little, until a soft dough is formed. Transfer to a lightly floured surface and knead until smooth, then roll into a ball. Using your fingertips, press the dough into a rectangle or circle shape (depending on the shape of the dish you are using) and then use a rolling pin or wine bottle to roll flat. Place in the greased pie dish. Trim the edges of the dough with kitchen scissors, leaving a 1½ cm (½ in) overhang.

Fold and crimp the edges of the overhanging pastry using your thumb and forefinger. Gather the pastry scraps into a ball, roll flat and then cut into little shapes to decorate the top later.

For the filling: In a large saucepan, heat 2 tablespoons of olive oil over a medium–high heat. Add the shallots and cook until translucent, about 2 minutes. Add the mushrooms and cook, stirring, until soft and cooked through, about 10 minutes. You may need to add a little water to the pan to stop them from sticking. Add the kale and cook until soft, about 2 minutes.

Meanwhile, place the remaining 4 tablespoons of olive oil in a large mixing bowl along with the remaining ingredients, except the basil leaves. Whisk until well combined and set aside.

Once the mushrooms and kale are cooked, pour them into the chickpea flour mixture and stir so that everything is well combined. Pour into the pastry-lined pie dish and decorate with the little pastry shapes.

Cook in the hot oven for 30 minutes, or until the middle of the quiche is firm when you press it with your forefinger.

Allow to cool for 10 minutes, then slice and devour. If you are planning to eat it later, allow it to cool in the dish at room temperature.

Serves 6-12

Shopping list
For the pastry crust:
coconut oil or vegan margarine
  for greasing
190 g (6½ oz/1½ cups) spelt
  flour, plus extra for dusting
½ teaspoon sea salt
4 tablespoons chilled coconut oil
  or vegan margarine
50-100 ml (2-3½ fl oz/
  3-5 tablespoons) water

For the filling:
6 tablespoons olive oil
2 shallots, thinly sliced
500 g (1 lb 2 oz) assorted
  mushrooms, such as shiitake,
  oyster, chanterelle, or whatever
  is available and affordable,
  cleaned and chopped
100 g (3½ oz) kale
250 g (9 oz/2 cups) chickpea flour
500 ml (17 fl oz/2 cups) water
6 tablespoons nutritional yeast
  (yeast flakes)
1 teaspoon black salt
1 teaspoon ground turmeric
1 teaspoon freshly ground
  black pepper
1 teaspoon onion powder
2 tablespoons finely chopped
  fresh chives
fresh basil leaves, to garnish

Maple Peanut Muesli Slice

This deliciously moreish muesli slice is good for snacks, transports easily for picnics and stores well, so you can make a big batch and have it in your pantry for impromptu hangs and healthy playdate treats. If you have nut allergies to account for, make this with sunflower-seed butter or tahini and replace the nuts with sunflower seeds.

Preheat the oven to 180°C (350°F/Gas 4). Line a deep baking tray (sheet), 20 x 30 cm (8 x 12 in), with baking paper.

Spread the oats, nuts and coconut over a separate baking tray and bake in the hot oven for 10 minutes, so they are lightly toasted.

Meanwhile, heat the peanut butter and maple syrup in a medium-large saucepan on a low heat, until the peanut butter has melted. Add the mashed dates and stir to combine. Add the toasted ingredients to the pan along with the puffed rice and vanilla. Stir to combine, then press into the lined deep baking tray in an even layer. Place in the refrigerator for 30 minutes to set.

Once the slice is set, remove from the refrigerator and cut into rectangles. Melt the chocolate chips in a small saucepan over a very low heat, drizzle over the slices to decorate and sprinkle with seeds, if using. Place the slices back in the refrigerator to set for about 10 minutes. Transfer to an airtight container and store in the refrigerator or pantry until ready to eat. They will keep for about 2 weeks (if they last that long!).

Makes about 18 slices

Shopping list

190 g (6½ oz/2 cups) rolled (old-fashioned) oats (use gluten-free if you need to)
125 g (4 oz/1 cup) chopped nuts, such as almonds, hazelnuts or pecans, roughly chopped
70 g (2½ oz/1 cup) shredded coconut
225 g (8 oz/1 cup) peanut butter
150 g (5 oz/½ cup) maple syrup
10 Medjool dates, pitted and mashed with a fork
30 g (1 oz/1 cup) puffed rice
1 teaspoon vanilla powder or extract
50 g (2 oz) vegan dark chocolate, to decorate
sesame seeds, to decorate (optional)

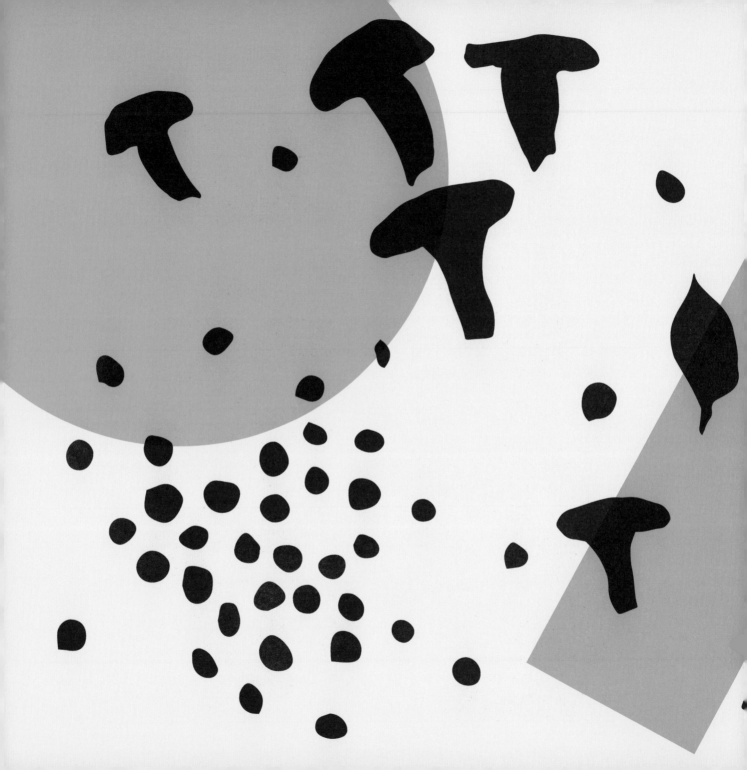

Grazing

& Finger Food

This is the food you can eat either before a meal or as a meal. Stuff that's good to whip up for unexpected guests, or when you realise you haven't made as much food as you thought you were going to. Stuff for your guests to nibble on while you finish cooking. Stuff for picnics and lazy grazy afternoons in the sunshine.

The Ultimate Grazing Table

People love a good grazing table. Mine are always built from an array of vegetables, fruits, nuts, seeds, legumes and herbs that have been chopped, cooked, seasoned and blended into an array of dips, spreads and nibbly things. Grazing tables can be served as an appetiser or starter to a bigger meal, or as the main meal itself, which is one of my favourite ways to eat during the warmer months.

Ingredients
When it comes to ingredients, make sure they are good quality, especially the olives. There's nothing worse than an olive that's taken on the flavour of all the other things inside the deli counter at the supermarket.

Don't be afraid to buy dips if you don't have time to make them all. There are some great-quality vegan goodies available these days – just know your brands and make sure you're aware of what all of the ingredients are, especially the ones that are listed as numbers.

Textures and flavours
Serve a mixture of textures and flavours: think soft, crunchy, sweet, salty, tart, creamy… Remember your gluten-intolerant friends. Fancy corn chips are a great one to serve, as are the seedy crackers from my first book.

Drinks
Don't forget something yummy to drink, such as the cocktails on pages 151–153, and water, lots of water.

Styling
When it comes to styling, start with a wooden board. Top with little bowls of dips, spreads, olives and berries. Add bread and crackers, fruit and pickled things. Fill any gaps with chocolate and more fruit, plus something leafy such as basil leaves or rocket (arugula). Cluster everything together and don't be afraid to let it spill off your board and onto the table. Add some little knives and spoons and include some cloth napkins or a tea towel for dirty fingers. Boom.

Sunshine
Crackers
(page 41)

Ajo
Blanco
(page 38)

Umami
Bomb Cashew
Spread
(page 39)

Mushroom
Pâté
(page 39)

Curried
Pumpkin
Hummus
(page 40)

4

Dips

(that aren't hummus)

All of these recipes were shown to me by or inspired by a special person in my life and all of them make an excellent addition to a grazing table. The Ajo Blanco is outrageous and a specialty of my friend Maria's family in Spain. The Spicy Capsicum Dip was created for my sister-in-law, who was missing her favourite supermarket brand of dip after finding out she can't eat lactose. The Umami Bomb Cashew Spread is an ode to the cheeseballs my mum used to make whenever she was having a party, and the Mushroom Pâté is inspired by a dip that a friend once brought to a potluck that blew our minds so much that I just had to recreate it.

Ajo Blanco

Shopping list
200 g (7 oz/1½ cups) blanched almonds
100 g (3½ oz) white bread (see Note)
2 garlic cloves, finely chopped
2 tablespoons olive oil
2 tablespoons white vinegar
½ teaspoon sea salt
250 ml (8½ fl oz/1 cup) ice-cold water
  or unsweetened almond milk
olive oil to serve

Preheat the oven to 180°C (350°F/Gas 4).
  Spread the almonds on a baking tray (sheet) and place in the hot oven for 3–5 minutes. Keep a close eye on them – you don't want them to turn brown, just to ever so slightly begin to toast. When you see little bubbles of oil starting to form on them, remove from the oven and allow to cool on the tray.
  Reserving a few of the almonds for garnish, place the rest in a high-speed blender, along with the bread, garlic, oil, vinegar, salt and half of the liquid. Purée until smooth, adding more liquid until you have a smooth runny dip (you may not need all of it). Serve immediately, garnished with a tiny drizzle of olive oil and some of the reserved almonds, sliced. Alternatively, transfer to an airtight container until ready to serve (it will keep for up to 5 days in the refrigerator).

Note: You want the bread to be good-quality white bread, but not sweet and not sour. I usually use a rustic Italian loaf from a nearby bakery. I cut it in half and then pluck out the white interior. Once the dip is ready, we scrape the blender clean with the crust.

Spicy Pepper Dip

Shopping list
125 g (4 oz/1 cup) cashews
190 ml (6 fl oz/⅔ cup) water
1 teaspoon freshly squeezed lemon juice
2 teaspoons sriracha sauce
2 garlic cloves
1 large red (bell) pepper, roasted
  (see Note below)
½ teaspoon sea salt
¼ teaspoon freshly ground black pepper

Place all the ingredients in a high-speed blender and process until smooth. If you don't own a high-speed blender, either soak the cashews in water overnight or boil them for 15 minutes, then drain – this will soften them and make it easier to get them nice and smooth.

Note: You can use a roasted pepper from a jar, or roast your own. To do this, pop a whole pepper in a 200°C (400°F/Gas 6) oven for 25 minutes, turning once during the cooking time. Transfer to a heatproof bowl, cover with a plate and set aside for 30 minutes. After this, the skin will easily slide off and you can remove the seeds and use the roasted pepper in your dip.

All dips serve 4–8 and can be served immediately, or stored in an airtight container in the fridge for up to 5 days.

Mushroom Pâté

Shopping list
1 tablespoon olive oil
2 shallots, finely chopped
300 g (10½ oz) mushrooms, finely chopped
2 garlic cloves, peeled and finely chopped
125 ml (4 fl oz/½ cup) white wine
2 bay leaves
1 teaspoon dried thyme
⅛ teaspoon ground nutmeg
½ teaspoon sea salt
½ teaspoon freshly ground black pepper
125 g (4 oz/1 cup) walnut halves,
   roughly chopped
1 tablespoon pine nuts
1 tablespoon balsamic vinegar
additional balsamic vinegar, to garnish
fresh thyme leaves, to garnish

Heat the olive oil in a frying pan (skillet) over a medium–high heat. Add the shallots and cook until translucent, about 5 minutes. Add the mushrooms, garlic, white wine, bay leaves, dried thyme, nutmeg, salt and pepper. Bring to a simmer, then lower the heat to medium and continue to cook, stirring now and again, until the white wine and liquid from the mushrooms has cooked off and the mushrooms are soft, about 20 minutes. Set aside to cool, then remove the bay leaves.

Meanwhile, toast the walnuts and pine nuts in a dry frying pan (skillet) over a medium heat, stirring frequently, for 5–10 minutes.

Transfer the cooked mushrooms and nuts to a food processor, reserving a few pine nuts for the top of the pâté. Add the balsamic vinegar and purée until you have an almost smooth paste with a few chunks to keep the texture interesting. Either enjoy immediately, garnished with a little balsamic vinegar and some fresh thyme leaves.

Umami Bomb Cashew Spread

Shopping list
125 g (4 oz/1 cup) cashews
1 teaspoon fenugreek seeds or
   4 sun-dried tomatoes, finely chopped
2 tablespoons nutritional yeast
1 teaspoon miso paste
1 teaspoon apple cider vinegar
½ teaspoon garlic powder
1 teaspoon sea salt
80 ml (2½ fl oz/⅓ cup) coconut oil, melted
black sesame seeds, to garnish

Soak the cashews and fenugreek seeds or sun-dried tomatoes in water overnight, or for a few hours at least. Drain, then place all the ingredients in a high-speed blender. Pulse a few times, then process until well combined.

Line a small plastic container or bowl with cling film (plastic wrap). Pour the mixture in, making sure to get all the bits from the side of the blender and under the blade. Pop it in the refrigerator for a few hours to let it firm up (it will take on the round shape of the bowl), then remove the cling film, roll the edges in the black sesame seeds and serve.

Hummus Revisited

I umm-ed and ahh-ed about whether to include hummus in this book, because I have a recipe for it in my first book and a recipe for it on my blog. Does the world really need another hummus recipe? After consulting with my editor, we agreed that hummus is such an important staple – for vegans and non-vegans alike – that it deserves its spot in book number two. Not only that, but it's my go-to when entertaining, an infinite crowd-pleaser and one of the easiest things to whip up when you have a large or small gathering to feed.

Also, since writing my first book, I've learned a little secret about how to make your hummus next-level creamy – you gotta peel the chickpeas! A tedious task if you're in a rush, but an enjoyable one if you sit down and relax into it. I've also become the proud owner of a high-speed blender and, I have to say, whilst I stand by my previous claim that delicious food can be made no matter how mediocre your kitchen setup is, I am truly amazed at how smooth and creamy my dips are now that I am using this beast of a machine.

If using tinned chickpeas, sit down and pop the chickpeas out of their skins, one by one. You can also put them in a tea towel and rub them around, which will loosen some of the skins and make them easier to peel off.

If cooking chickpeas from scratch, soak overnight in warm water, then drain and rinse. Cover with fresh water and add 1 teaspoon barcarbonate of soda, then simmer for 30–40 minutes (depends on freshness of chickpeas), checking from time to time, until tender. Most of the skins will float to the surface. Scoop them away with a slotted spoon and give the pan a stir, scooping away the new skins that float to the surface. Continue until you've got all those pesky skins.

Place the chickpeas and tahini in a high-speed blender and blend until the chickpeas are smooth. Add the remaining ingredients, along with half the ice-cold water. Blend until well combined, adding more water until your desired consistency is reached (you may not need it all). Enjoy as it is, or try one of my favourite variations below:

Curried pumpkin: add up to 135 g (4½ oz/1 cup) cooked pumpkin and 1 generous tablespoon curry powder.

Beetroot (beet) and horseradish: add 1 large cooked beetroot (beet) and 1 generous teaspoon horseradish paste.

Chipotle lime: use lime instead of lemon juice and add 1 tablespoon chipotle paste or 1 chipotle pepper in adobo sauce. Serve with corn chips for a Mexican-inspired feast.

Serves 4-8

Shopping list

400 g (14 oz) tin cooked chickpeas (garbanzo beans), drained and rinsed (or ¾ cup dried chickpeas, soaked overnight, drained, then cooked from scratch with 1 teaspoon bicarbonate of soda (baking soda – see method)
3–4 generous tablespoons tahini
1 garlic clove, peeled and roughly chopped
juice of ½ lemon
1 tablespoon olive oil
1 teaspoon ground cumin
½ teaspoon ground coriander
½ teaspoon fine sea salt
250 ml (8½ fl oz/1 cup) ice-cold water

Sunshine Crackers

These little bites of sunshine are an adaptation of my mum's cheese straw recipe. I first made them because it was difficult to find such crackers in Berlin, but they fast became a staple in our home because Louie is utterly obsessed with them. They are light and crumbly with a mild curry flavour, which makes them perfect for dipping or for eating on their own.

Preheat the oven to 180°C (350°F/Gas 4).

Place the dry ingredients in a food processor and pulse to combine. Add the margarine or coconut oil and pulse some more. Turn the food processor to a low speed, then slowly pour in the water, splash by splash (you may not need it all). All of a sudden, you will have a ball of dough.

Transfer the dough to a sheet of baking paper. Knead a couple of times, then press into a flat disc. Cover with another sheet of baking paper and then use a rolling pin to roll the dough out until it's about 3 mm (⅛ in) thick. Transfer to a baking tray (sheet), then remove the top sheet of baking paper. Cut into little shapes, as close together as possible. Remove the inverse section of the dough, leaving your little shapes behind on the tray. Pop in the hot oven for 10 minutes. While that batch is cooking, roll out and makes some more shapes with the remaining dough. You can also cut them into sticks, if you prefer.

Once cooked, remove from oven and allow to fully cool on the tray. Enjoy immediately or store in an airtight jar until ready to eat (they will keep for up to 2 weeks).

Note: If you are gluten intolerant, there's a great recipe for gluten-free 'seedy crackers' in my first book!

Serves 4-8

Shopping list
125 g (4 oz/1 cup) spelt flour
65 g (2¼ oz/½ cup) chickpea (gram) flour
35 g (1¼ oz/¼ cup) nutritional yeast (yeast flakes)
1 heaped tablespoon curry powder
2 teaspoons baking powder
heaped ¼ teaspoon salt
3 tablespoons vegan margarine or coconut oil
125 ml (4 fl oz/½ cup) cold water

Mushroom & Jackfruit Party Pies

In Australia and New Zealand, 'party pies' are a staple of children's birthday parties. Traditionally they are filled with minced (ground) meat, but I've filled mine with the winning combo of mushrooms and jackfruit. I use store-bought puff pastry - I've been harbouring a mini obsession with it since finding out that most puff pastry is in fact vegan. No, it's not a wholefood and it's got pretty much zero nutritional value, but goddamn it's delicious and that makes it good for the soul. Just be sure to buy a brand that doesn't contain palm oil and is preferably organic.

Preheat the oven to 200°C (400°F/Gas 6) and line a baking tray (sheet) with baking paper.

Heat the oil in a large frying pan (skillet) over a medium heat. Add the shallot and cook for 2-3 minutes, then add the mushrooms and cook for about 5 minutes, until soft. Meanwhile, cut the tough bits off the jackfruit and set aside. Crumble the soft jackfruit pieces into the pan. Finely chop the tough bits and add to the pan, along with the tomato paste and maple syrup, and stir to combine. In a small bowl, combine the spices, herbs, salt, flour and milk to make a gravy, stirring until no clumps remain. Add the gravy to the mushrooms and jackfruit, and cook for about 2 minutes, stirring, until the mixture has thickened and is well combined.

Cut each puff pastry sheet into 4 smaller squares. Take a square of pastry and place 1 generous teaspoon of filling on top, positioning it to one side of the centre. Fold the other side of the pastry over to encase the filling, then crimp the edges with a fork to seal. Gently transfer the pie to the lined baking tray and poke generous holes in the top of each pie with a small, sharp knife (the holes will reduce in size as the pastry puffs up).

Repeat, until all of your filling and pastry is used up, then brush the tops of the pies with milk. Bake in the hot oven for 15-20 minutes, or until puffed up and golden. The final cooking time will depend on the brand of puff pastry, which varies from country to country. Check the packet for guidance.

Enjoy warm or cold, dunked in good old-fashioned tomato ketchup.

Makes 16 pies

Shopping list

1 tablespoon olive oil
1 shallot, finely chopped
250 g (9 oz) brown mushrooms, finely chopped
565 g (20 oz) tin jackfruit in brine, drained and rinsed
2 tablespoons tomato paste
1 tablespoon maple syrup
1 teaspoon onion powder
1 teaspoon garlic granules
½ teaspoon ground coriander
½ teaspoon freshly ground black pepper
¾ teaspoon dried thyme
¾ teaspoon sea salt
2 tablespoons plain (all-purpose) flour
125 ml (4 fl oz/½ cup) plant-based milk, plus additional milk for brushing
4 (30 x 30-cm/12 x 12-in) sheets puff pastry

To serve:
tomato ketchup

Antipasti Skewers

This recipe is designed for those times when you want to make something for a picnic or gathering, but don't have time to get all fancy pants and make every single component from scratch. The old me would have scoffed at such a recipe, but the new me - the mum me - the more in touch with the real world me - knows that cooking everything from scratch all the time is a luxury that is not available to everyone, and that using store-bought gnocchi does not make you a lesser cook by any means.

Cook the gnocchi according to the packet instructions. Drain, rinse with cold water and then place in a large mixing bowl. Drizzle with olive oil and shake around so the gnocchi pieces are all individually coated in the oil. Taste for seasoning - depending on the brand you buy, you may need to ever so lightly salt your gnocchi.

Wrap 1 tomato half with 1 basil leaf and *carefully* thread onto a skewer, followed by 1 gnocchi piece and 1 olive. Repeat once or twice, so that you have 2-3 pieces of each ingredient on each skewer. Repeat until you've used up all the ingredients, placing the completed skewers on a serving platter.

Dress the skewers with freshly cracked black pepper and Balsamic Reduction. They are best eaten immediately or a few hours after making, but you can store in the refrigerator for up to half a day (make in the morning to eat in the evening).

Note: Its worth buying the best quality gnocchi you can find, and definitely gnocchi that's stored in the fridge at the supermarket as opposed to the stuff you find on the shelf. Also, it goes without saying but if you're vegan, make sure the variety of gnocchi you purchase does not contain egg.

To make 20 x 20 cm (8 in) skewers

Shopping list
60 pieces of gnocchi (I use a
   400 g/14 oz packet)
1 tablespoon high-quality olive oil
30 mini Roma (Italian plum)
   tomatoes, halved
60 basil leaves
60 Kalamata olives, stones removed
salt and freshly ground black
   pepper to taste

To serve:
Balsamic Reduction (page 121)

Pumpkin & Black Bean Rollups

I'm obsessed with all things pumpkin and these crispy, tasty morsels never fail to please. They make an excellent starter or snack, or you can turn them into a meal by serving them with some BBQ'd corn and a simple side salad.

Heat 1 tablespoon canola oil in a medium saucepan over a medium heat. Add the onion and cook until lightly browned. Add the mashed pumpkin, black beans, coriander (cilantro) and spices and stir to combine.

Heat the remaining tablespoon of canola oil in a large frying pan (skillet) over a medium–high heat. Spread 1 tablespoon of the pumpkin and black bean filling onto each tortilla and roll up. Place the rollups in the hot oil, seam side down, and fry until golden, turning frequently until the tortillas are crispy and golden brown all over. Depending on the size of your pan, you should be able to do 2–3 at a time. Transfer to paper towels while you cook the others.

To serve, stack the rollups on top of one another, drizzle with a little Cashew Cream and top with Pickled Jalapeños and coriander (cilantro) leaves. Serve the remaining cashew cream on the side for dunking.

Serves 4-8

Shopping list

2 tablespoons canola oil
1 small white onion,
    finely chopped
135 g (4½ oz/1 cup) pumpkin,
    cooked and puréed or mashed
    until smooth
400 g (14 oz) tin black beans,
    drained and rinsed
10 g (½ oz/¼ cup) finely chopped
    coriander (cilantro) leaves
1 teaspoon ground coriander
½ teaspoon sea salt
½ teaspoon garlic granules
8 tortilla wraps (a corn/wheat
    blend is best here)

To serve:
Chipotle Cashew Cream
    (page 120)
Quick Pickled Jalapeños
    (page 116)
fresh coriander (cilantro) leaves
fresh lime, to sqeeze

Bruschetta Forever

Bruschetta are perfect either as a starter, or as an all-afternoon/evening grazing affair. I like to prep everything and lay it out beautifully for my guests, so that they can build their own bruschetta as they please. This not only encourages the fun of interaction with food, but prevents the bread from going soggy.

For the bruschetta: Cut your bread into 1 cm (½ in) slices. Toast in a 180°C (350°F/Gas 4) oven or a sandwich press for 4–5 minutes, then allow to cool. (You may need to do this in batches while you prep the other ingredients.) Once cool, rub one side of each bruschetta piece with the garlic clove and drizzle or brush with olive oil. Place on a wooden serving board with one or all of the following toppings.

For the cherry tomato topping: Place the olive oil in a large frying pan (skillet) over a medium heat. Add the shallot and cook until soft, about 2 minutes. Add the cherry tomatoes, balsamic vinegar and salt and cook until the tomatoes start to become soft but still hold their form, about 3–4 minutes. Remove from heat, allow to cool and season with black pepper to taste.

For the green pea pesto: For a smooth pesto, place everything in a high-speed food processor and purée until smooth. Alternatively, for a chunky pesto, proceed as above, but only use half the peas initially. Once smooth, add the remaining peas and pulse just a few times to combine.

For the garlic white beans: Place everything in a small mixing bowl and stir to combine.

Serves 4–8

Shopping list
Bruschetta:
1 large baguette
1 large garlic clove, peeled
   and halved
olive oil for drizzling

Cherry tomato topping:
1 tablespoon olive oil
1 small shallot, diced
25–30 cherry tomatoes, halved
1 teaspoon balsamic vinegar
1 teaspoon fine salt
freshly ground black pepper
   to taste

Green pea pesto:
250 g (9 oz/2 cups) frozen peas,
   defrosted
30 g (1 oz/1 cup) tightly packed
   basil leaves
60 ml (2 fl oz/¼ cup) olive oil
60 ml (2 fl oz/¼ cup) freshly
   squeezed lemon juice (1 lemon)
2–3 garlic cloves, peeled
   and finely chopped
½ teaspoon salt

Garlic white beans:
400 g (14 oz) tin cannellini beans,
   drained and rinsed
4 tablespoons Garlic Mayo
   (page 115)
½ small red onion, thinly sliced
salt and freshly ground black
   pepper to taste

Additional toppings:
fresh basil leaves
rocket (arugula)
Balsamic Reduction (page 121)
Cashew Ricotta (page 124)

Baked Almond Feta with Balsamic-Roasted Grapes

This recipe was shared with me by the folks at Vegan Apron and it is absolutely to die for. When I made it as part of a cheese board for my very un-vegan family at Christmas time, no one could believe it was vegan. It takes a couple of days to make the cheese from start to finish, but the outcome is so divine, it is well worth the effort.

For the baked almond feta: Soak the almonds in cold water overnight, or boil in a small saucepan of water for 15 minutes. Drain and rinse. Place the soaked almonds in a high-speed blender, along with the cold water, lemon juice, olive oil, garlic, salt and nutritional yeast, and process until smooth. Transfer the mixture to a mixing bowl.

In a small pan, dissolve the agar agar powder in the warm water, bring to the boil, then reduce the heat and simmer for 2–3 minutes. Remove from the heat and whisk into the almond mixture, along with the dried herbs, apple cider vinegar and lemon zest.

Line a small, rounded bowl with cheesecloth (muslin) and spoon the almond mixture into the cheesecloth, smoothing out the top with the back of a spoon. Fold over the edges of the cheesecloth to cover and chill in the refrigerator overnight.

The next day, preheat the oven to 190°C (375°F/Gas 5) and line a baking tray (sheet) with baking paper.

Gently remove the cheesecloth and transfer the almond feta to the baking tray. Bake for 40 minutes, until lightly golden and the top is firm.

For the balsamic-roasted grapes: Toss the grapes in the oil, balsamic vinegar, salt, pepper and thyme leaves, then transfer to a roasting dish (pan). Roast in the hot oven for 15 minutes (ideally when the almond feta has been in the oven for 25 minutes, so they are both ready at the same time).

Allow to cool, then transfer the baked almond feta to a serving dish, top with the roasted grapes and garnish with a few thyme sprigs. Serve with crusty bread.

Serves 4–8

Shopping list
Baked almond feta:
250 g (9 oz/scant 2 cups)
   blanched almonds
120 ml (4 fl oz/½ cup) cold water
juice of 1 lemon
3 tablespoons olive oil
1 garlic clove, peeled
1 teaspoon sea salt
1 tablespoon nutritional yeast
   (yeast flakes)
1 teaspoon agar agar powder
60 ml (2 fl oz/¼ cup) warm water
2 teaspoons dried oregano
1 teaspoon dried thyme
1 teaspoon apple cider vinegar
grated zest of ½ lemon

Balsamic-roasted grapes:
1 large bunch red grapes
1 tablespoon olive oil
1 tablespoon balsamic vinegar
sea salt and freshly ground
   black pepper to taste
a few sprigs fresh thyme leaves,
   plus extra to garnish

Cooking with an open flame imparts a sweet and smoky flavour to your food that makes it an intrinsic part of cultures all over the world. Coming from the southern hemisphere, BBQ grilling is synonymous with long summer nights and Christmas holidays – but as it doesn't get very cold in my hometown, it was commonplace for us to use the BBQ all year round.

I talk about my mum a lot when it comes to my relationship with cooking, but my dad was a great cook too. I have strong memories of him being outside, beer in hand, surrounded by friends, cooking up a feast on the grill to accompany the tableful of salads that he and my mum had prepared earlier. These days, he's still a deft hand at the BBQ, but since I've gotten all crazy over vegetables, the things he cooks on it have changed somewhat.

Veggies are often overlooked by avid grillers in favour of meat, and what a crying shame that is because the humble vegetable is effortlessly transformed when cooked on hot metal and open fire. My go-tos are corn and asparagus, but you can cook pretty much any vegetable on a grill and it doesn't stop there – tofu, fruit, bread and even cake make for delicious grilled fare.

In this chapter I'm sharing some of my favourite things to pop on a grill, ideas that have made my friends jump for joy and piqued the interested of many an omnivore.

I also wanted to share my thoughts about waste. I often see outdoor BBQ spots littered with disposable tableware. While it's not always possible to go entirely waste-free, a little thought and pre-planning can make a world of difference to our poor Mother Earth. Buy plates that you can use again and again and, if you must buy disposable ones, make sure they are bio-degradable at least (look for bamboo, most paper ones are covered in plastic). If you're hosting a feast, tell guests to BYO their own reusable plates, cups, cutlery and napkins.

When transporting food, avoid cling film (plastic wrap) in place of a tea towel or a plate on top of a bowl. My mum has reusable bowl covers that look like clear shower caps for different-sized heads, and beeswax wraps (not vegan, I know) are taking the world by storm at the moment, they are amazing! The same goes for aluminum foil and pans. Sometimes it's unavoidable, especially if you're squeamish about your veg food touching meat (I am), but be mindful. I use foil to bake sweet potatoes on the grill, but avoid all other disposable tools in favour of reusable ones.

The Beloved

BBQ

BBQ-Baked Sweet Potatoes with Jackfruit & Grilled Corn

Stringy jackfruit strikes again. Unparalleled in its ability to take on the texture and flavours of pulled meat, it has taken the vegan world by storm over the past few years. In this recipe, I bake sweet potatoes on the hot grill before stuffing them with cabbage, carrot, jackfruit and corn and topping them with creamy and spicy condiments. YUM!

Preheat the BBQ 20 minutes ahead of cooking.

Scrub each sweet potato clean, dry with a tea towel and prick a few times with a fork. Tightly wrap each potato individually in foil and place on the hot BBQ for 1 hour, turning once during the cooking time. After 1 hour, give them a squeeze with some tongs – they should feel soft. Remove from the heat and allow to rest for 15 minutes.

Meanwhile, drain the jackfruit and squeeze out as much brine as possible. Break the soft stringy bits of jackfruit away from the small, tough piece, discarding the seed pods as you go (they are perfectly edible but I prefer not to cook them). Combine the stringy pieces of jackfruit in a bowl with the BBQ sauce and set aside.

In a separate bowl, combine the cabbage and carrot and set aside. Slather the corn cob in the coconut oil and grill on the BBQ, turning it as it cooks, until slightly blackened all over. Heat the jackfruit, either directly on the flat-plate part of the grill (if you have one), in a cast-iron pan, or on top of some foil.

When everything is ready, carefully remove the foil from the potatoes. Cut through the skin along the top of the potatoes with a sharp knife and push the soft, cooked flesh to the sides with a fork, to make room for the fillings. Start with the red cabbage and carrot, then top with the jackfruit sauce. Cut the corn away from the cob and sprinkle this over. Finally, add a generous dollop of Chipotle Cashew Cream/sour cream/yoghurt, a sprinkling of coriander (cilantro) leaves and jalapeños.

Note: You can also make these in the oven. I turn it to the highest heat, cook the foil-wrapped potatoes for 30 minutes, then turn off the oven, leaving the potatoes to cook in the residual heat for another 30 minutes–2 hours. If kept in the foil, they will stay warm for hours.

Hot Tip! If you want to enjoy this recipe but don't want to wait an hour for the sweet potatoes to cook, heat some tortillas on the grill (griddle) and fill with all the fillings for some seriously killer tacos.

Serves 4

Shopping list
4 sweet potatoes, about
   450 g (1 lb) each
565 g (20 oz) tin jackfruit in
   brine (drained weight about
   300 g (10½ oz))
125 ml (4 fl oz/½ cup) BBQ
   sauce (either from a bottle
   or see recipe on page 121)
¼ head red cabbage, shredded
1 carrot, peeled and sliced
1 corn cob
1 tablespoon coconut oil

To serve:
Chipotle Cashew Cream
   (page 120), vegan
   sour cream or coconut yoghurt
large handful coriander (cilantro)
   leaves, roughly chopped
lots of Quick Pickled Jalapeños
   (page 116)

Marinated Tofu 3 Ways

People love to make fun of tofu, especially when there are sausages involved. Yet every time I make this tofu - especially if it's in skewer form - they swarm and drool, beg for a taste, then beg for the recipe, because they can't believe it's possible to make tofu taste so good. I'm sharing this in the BBQ chapter, but it's equally good baked in the oven, if you don't have easily accessible grilling facilities.

Cut the tofu according to how you wish to enjoy it.

 **For tofu skewers:** cut in approximately 1½ cm (⅝ in) cubes. These are good if you are cooking on a grill with a widely spaced grate.

For tofu pieces: you can work with the size of the block. Cut it in half and then into pieces that are about ½ cm (¼ in) wide each. These are good if you are cooking on the flat-plate part of a BBQ.

For tofu steaks: cut the entire block into ½ cm (¼ in) long slabs. These are good on both the grate and flat-plate.

Put all the marinade ingredients in a shallow dish and whisk to combine. Place the tofu in the marinade and set aside to marinate for as long as possible – 30 minutes is fine, but overnight is even better. I usually leave it out on the worktop while I am cooking, so I remember to give it a swirl every so often, to make sure all the tofu gets evenly coated in the marinade, then I pop it in the refrigerator overnight, covered.

If making skewers, thread the tofu onto skewers (if using wooden skewers, soak them in water first), about 6–8 pieces per skewer. If transporting to a BBQ, pop the completed skewers in a large plastic container along with any additional marinade, so that they are ready to go once you arrive.

Preheat the BBQ 20 minutes ahead of cooking. Cook the marinated tofu (skewers, pieces or steaks) on a hot BBQ for 2–3 minutes each side, or until slightly blackened on some parts. Serve with Almond Butter Satay Sauce, either on top of a noodle salad, alongside some grilled veggies, or in a flatbread with cucumber and salad.

Hot Tip! If you want to enjoy this outrageously good tofu without a BBQ, bake the tofu on a baking tray (sheet) in a 190°C (375°F/Gas 5) oven for 20 minutes, then pop them on top of a salad. Heaven.

Serves 4-8

Shopping list
400 g (14 oz) firm tofu, drained and pressed for at least 30 minutes
Almond Butter Satay Sauce (page 120)

Marinade:
2 tablespoons rice vinegar
2 tablespoons tamari
1 tablespoon sesame oil
1 teaspoon sriracha sauce
1 teaspoon grated fresh ginger
1 teaspoon grated garlic

Grilling Everything Else

As already mentioned, you can put pretty much any vegetable on the BBQ. Corn is good with just a bit of coconut oil smeared on it first, then some chimichurri or pesto smeared on it afterwards. Asparagus is also good with just a quick sear and a squeeze of lemon and sprinkle of salt to dress it. Cauliflower steaks, snow peas, mushrooms and courgettes (zucchini) are even better with a marinade. The Best of the Best Marinade goes very well with tofu (and anything, really), and one of my more recent discoveries, Chimichurri Sauce, is an excellent way to add some tangy freshness to sweet and smoky charred veggies.

The Best of the Best Marinade

Makes 180 ml (6 fl oz/¾ cup)

Shopping list
60 ml (2 fl oz/¼ cup) tamari
60 ml (2 fl oz/¼ cup) rice vinegar
2 tablespoons sesame oil
1 tablespoon sriracha sauce

Mix together all the ingredients in a bowl. Toss vegetables in the marinade and allow to sit for 30 minutes before cooking on a hot grill.

Chimichurri Sauce

Makes about 250 ml (8½ fl oz/1 cup)

Shopping list
40 g (1½ oz/1 cup) tightly packed
   coriander (cilantro) leaves
20 g (¾ oz/½ cup) tightly packed
   parsley leaves
1 tablespoon fresh oregano
1 garlic clove, peeled
60 ml (2 fl oz/¼ cup) olive oil
juice of 1 lime
1 teaspoon maple syrup
½ teaspoon sea salt

Place all the ingredients in a high-speed food processor and pulse until smooth. Store in an airtight jar until ready to use It will keep for 2 days. (See photo overleaf.)

BBQ'd Flatbread

Nothing beats the taste and texture of fresh bread, especially when it's been cooked on a hot grill (griddle). You can use this to tear and dunk into dips, wrap around marinated tofu topped with cucumber and satay sauce, or to make a delicious grilled veggie sandwich.

Makes 6 × 18 cm (7 in) flatbreads

Shopping list
320 g (11½ oz/2½ cups) plain (all-purpose) flour, plus extra for dusting
2 teaspoons instant yeast (dry active)
250 ml (8½ fl oz/1 cup) warm water
1 tablespoon sesame oil, plus extra for oiling
¾ teaspoon sea salt
3–4 spring onions (scallions), finely chopped

In a large mixing bowl, combine 60 g (2 oz/½ cup) of the flour with the yeast and warm water. Set aside until the mixture becomes bubbly, then add the remaining flour, sesame oil, salt and spring onions (scallions). Knead in the bowl for 2–3 minutes, then cover with a tea towel and allow to sit in a warm place for 1 hour or until the dough has doubled in size.

Preheat the BBQ 20 minutes ahead of cooking. Divide the dough into 6 balls and roll out to a thickness of 5 mm (¼ in) on a lightly floured surface. Spray or wipe a little oil onto the flat-plate. Add the bread and cook for 2–3 minutes, until big bubbles start to form on the uncooked side, then flip and cook for 2–3 minutes until slightly golden. When cooked, stack on top of one another and wrap in a clean tea towel.

Allow them to rest for 30 minutes–1 hour, or until ready to use. This will keep them soft and easy to wrap around the rest of your yummies. (See photo overleaf.)

Potato & Sauerkraut Fritters

After living in Germany for five years, I developed a sauerkraut addiction. I love it so much, I eat it straight out of the jar, much to Andy's disgust. Germans love sauerkraut too, so much that they sell its juice by the carton in stores. I do love my kraut but I can't say I've ever felt compelled to try it in juice form... These little fritters take the tang and crunch of sauerkraut and fry it into crispy little bites of heaven, that you can nibble away on as is, or pop into a sandwich with salad and mayo and other yum things.

Makes 8 fritters

Shopping list
140 g (4½ oz/1 cup) diced potato, cooked until soft in salted water
120 g (4 oz/1 cup) tightly packed sauerkraut or kimchi, plus some juice from the jar
60 g (2 oz/½ cup) rice flour
½ teaspoon baking powder
coconut oil for cooking

Preheat the flat-plate part of a BBQ for 20 minutes before cooking. Meanwhile, mash the potato with a little bit of juice from the sauerkraut jar (no need to buy a whole carton here haha!). Once your potato is mostly smooth with a few lumps remaining, stir through the rice flour and baking powder, then add the sauerkraut and stir to combine.

Wipe the hot flat-plate with a little coconut oil. Place tablespoons of fritter mix onto the hot surface and flatten with the back of the spoon so that each fritter is about 1 cm (½ in) deep. Cook for 2 minutes or until golden brown on the underside, then flip and cook for another 2 minutes. Repeat until all the batter is used up.

Chimichurri
Sauce
(page 58)

Marinated
Tofu *(page 57)*
with BBQ'd
flatbread
(page 59)

Meals to
Build Together

This chapter is about those meals where you prepare lots of different bits and pieces beforehand, then serve up casually, so that everyone can have a turn at building their own delicious little creations. Such affairs are almost always fun, messy and hilarious, and they allow guests to eat according to their appetite.

This chapter is also handy for times when you want to host a feast but don't have the time or budget to make everything in each recipe. You and your guests can share the tasks amongst yourselves and bring it all together around the dinner table.

Black Bean and Crumbed-Cauliflower Tacos

Black beans and crumbed cauliflower, topped with creamy cashews, tangy pickled onions and sweet pineapple salsa, and enveloped by warm corn tortillas – this is slow food at its finest. These vegan tacos have been hailed by vegans and meat-eaters alike as some of the best tacos they have ever eaten. They are perfect for a group of friends who meet often for dinner.

Reminiscent of popcorn chicken, the crumbed cauliflower is one of my favourite creations to date. It's a wee bit labour-intensive, so pour yourself a drink, sit down and relax into the task – it's worth it I promise.

Whilst this is my favourite taco recipe of all time, you don't have to stick to this recipe if you want to branch out and make the chunky salsa from my first book instead of the Grilled Pineapple Salsa (page 121), or the BBQ Jackfruit (page 54) instead of the cauliflower. Get creative, enjoy yourselves and don't forget the Spicy Ginger Margaritas (page 151)!

Serves 4–8

Shopping list
For the black beans:
500 g (1 lb 2 oz/3⅓ cups) dried black beans
1 tablespoon salt
1 brown onion, finely chopped
3 garlic cloves, peeled and finely chopped
2 tablespoons coriander (cilantro) stalks, finely chopped

For the crumbed cauliflower:
1 head cauliflower
olive oil, for brushing
125 g (4 oz/1 cup) plain (all-purpose) flour (use rice or buckwheat flour to make it gluten-free)
250 ml (8½ fl oz/1 cup) soy or plant-based milk
1 teaspoon salt
2 tablespoons each coriander seeds, cumin seeds, sesame seeds and hemp seeds (or whatever you have on hand)
50 g (2 oz/2 cups) cornflakes, crushed, or 80 g (3 oz/2 cups) panko breadcrumbs
1 teaspoon garlic powder
additional salt to taste

To serve:
Corn Tortillas (page 123)
Chipotle Cashew Cream (page 120) or Cashew Ricotta (page 124), or both
Grilled Pineapple Salsa (page 121)
Pink Pickled Onions (page 116)
baby tomatoes
fresh lime wedges
fresh coriander (cilantro) leaves
fresh red chillies, sliced
avocado (optional)

For the black beans: The secret to the best-ever black beans is to cook them from scratch, without soaking. You gotta trust me on this – they take longer, but only a little bit of their cooking time actually requires any work, so you can let them do their thing while you are preparing the rest of this feast.

Rinse and check over your beans to make sure that there are no sticks or stones lurking in your future dinner. Place the beans in a medium saucepan and cover with about 2½ cm (1 in) water. Place the saucepan over a high heat, bring to the boil and then lower to a simmer. Add the salt and allow to simmer away, topping up frequently with warm water, until the beans are soft. Mine are usually soft within 1½ hours, but they can take up to 2 hours.

Once the beans are soft, add the onion, garlic and coriander (cilantro) stalks to the pan. Allow the beans to continue cooking until they are thick and mushy and sticking to the bottom of the pan a little. Remove from the heat and allow to cool for about 20 minutes, before transferring to a high-speed blender and puréeing until smooth. (You can also purée them in the pot using an immersion blender if you don't have a high-speed blender.) Transfer the smooth beans to a small pan or serving dish and cover with a lid until ready to serve. Depending on how far in advance you make them, you may need to reheat before serving. If you've prepared the day before, add a little water before reheating as they will thicken overnight.

For the crumbed cauliflower: Remove the leaves from the cauliflower, then break the cauliflower into florets, and then into smaller florets, trimming off but not discarding the stems (they are also very tasty). You want each cauliflower piece to be about thumb-nail sized.

Preheat the oven to 190°C (375°F/Gas 5). Brush a large baking tray (sheet) or roasting dish (pan) with a little olive oil. In a small bowl, whisk together the flour, milk and salt to form a batter and set aside.

Using a mortar and pestle (or food processor), crush the seeds a little, then transfer to a wide, deep dish. I use a pasta bowl, but a lasagna dish would also work. Add the crushed cornflakes or panko breadcrumbs to the seeds, along with the garlic powder, and mix to combine.

Working in batches, coat the cauliflower pieces in batter, allow the batter to drip off a little, then toss the pieces in the crumb mix and place them on the oiled tray. I like to put about 3 pieces into the batter, remove them with a slotted spoon and let them sit for a second. You can also place a colander over a bowl and let the pieces drip off in there. Once all the pieces are coated, sprinkle them with salt and place the tray in the hot oven. Cook for 20–25 minutes, until golden. Serve immediately, or make ahead of time and reheat in a hot oven for 10 minutes before serving.

To serve:
Heat the tortillas and arrange all the individual ingredients in little serving bowls. Serve everything at the table, tell your guests what's there and let them build their own.

Chipotle
Cashew Cream
(page 120)

Corn
Tortillas
(page 123)

Grilled
Pineapple Salsa
(page 121)

Black-Bean and Crumbed-Cauliflower Tacos (page 64)

Top: Spicy Ginger Margarita (page 151); Bottom: Cashew Ricotta (page 124)

Rainbow Chard & Mushroom Dumplings

Makes about 40 dumplings (enough to feed 4–8, depending on what else you are serving)

Shopping list
For the dumpling dough:
250 g (9 oz/2 cups) plain (all-purpose) flour
1 teaspoon fine sea salt
215 ml (6½ fl oz/¾ cup) warm water

For the filling:
2 tablespoons sesame oil (canola or olive oil will also work)
500 g (1 lb 2 oz) fresh shiitake mushrooms (or whatever other mushrooms are affordable and available)
1 large or 2 small bunches chard, stalks removed and finely chopped (keep a few large leaves aside to line the steamer)
20 g (1 oz/½ cup) fresh coriander (cilantro) leaves, finely chopped
3–4 spring onions (scallions), finely chopped
4 garlic cloves, peeled and finely chopped
2 cm (¾ in) piece fresh ginger, grated
4 tablespoons sesame seeds
2 tablespoons tamari
1 tablespoon maple syrup
½ teaspoon salt

For the dipping sauce:
60 ml (2 fl oz/¼ cup) tamari
60 ml (2 fl oz/¼ cup) rice vinegar
1 fresh chilli, sliced (optional)

Another blog favourite, this is a recipe I developed years ago that has remained a loyal part of my repertoire. In our early Berlin years, when drinking always went hand-in-hand with dinner parties, I would prepare the filling and dough in advance and then we would sit around the table and play a game of 'make a dumpling, sip your sake' with friends, before steaming them and devouring our creations. As with any group-cooking activity that involves alcohol, hilarity always ensued.

I used to be intimidated at the thought of making my own dumpling dough, but let me say it is a lot easier than you might imagine and a kazillion times tastier. If you're not ready for such adventures, you can pick up dumpling dough in the freezer section of your Asian supermarket, just make sure to buy a brand that doesn't contain egg, and check how many wrappers are in each packet, you might need to grab two!

For the dumpling dough: Place the flour and salt in a large mixing bowl. Add the warm water and stir to combine, then transfer to a clean surface and knead until silky smooth, about 2 minutes. If the dough seems dry, add more warm water, 1 tablespoon at a time. Likewise, if it seems too wet, add a little flour, 1 teaspoon at a time, until the dough is silky smooth and neither sticky nor dry. Pop it back in the bowl, then cover with a plate and a tea towel, which will allow the warm water to fully hydrate the flour, making it lovely to work with when you are ready.

For the filling: Place a large saucepan over a low heat and add the sesame oil. Chop the mushrooms into tiny pieces, about 2-5 mm (⅛-¼ in), adding to the pot as you go and stirring occasionally, then add the chard. The mushrooms and chard will look like a lot at first but will shrink as they cook. Add the remaining ingredients and increase the heat to medium. Cook for 15-20 minutes, stirring frequently, until all ingredients are well-cooked and the liquid has evaporated off.

For the dipping sauce: Combine all ingredients and set aside. If you or any of your guests are sensitive to chilli, leave it out, or split the dipping sauce into two bowls and only add chilli to one.

To construct: Split the ball of dough in two and roll it out to a thickness of 2 mm (⅛ in). Using a cookie cutter or a glass, cut the dough into circles about 10 cm (4 in) in diameter. Place 1 teaspoon of filling into the centre of each circle, then wet the edges and fold the dough over the filling. Here, you can crimp the edges if you like but I prefer to take the corners and fold them round onto themselves (rather like Italian tortellini), as this makes the dumplings take up less space, which means you can fit more into the steamer basket. Repeat, until you have used up all the dough and all the filling.

To cook: Line the steamer basket with the reserved chard leaves. Place the dumplings in the basket, making sure they don't touch, otherwise they will stick together. Place the steamer basket over an appropriately sized pan of boiling water. Cover with the lid and steam for 5-10 minutes, until the wrappers are slightly transparent (be careful of the steam when checking).

Serve immediately, with dipping sauce. We usually make more while the first ones are cooking, then eat the first round while the second round is cooking and so on and so on until they are all gone and we are happy and silly and full. (See photo overleaf).

Rainbow Chard
& Mushroom
Dumplings
(pages 68-69)

Sesame-Mushroom Sushi

Makes 80 pieces of sushi, which will serve 4-8

Shopping list
For sesame-crusted mushrooms:
3 large portobello, shiitake
 or oyster mushrooms
60 g (2 oz/½ cup) plain
 (all-purpose) flour
60 g (2 oz/½ cup) rice flour
1 teaspoon baking powder
1 teaspoon salt
250 ml (8½ fl oz/1 cup) water
75 g (2½ oz/½ cup) black
 sesame seeds
150 g (5 oz/1 cup) white
 sesame seeds
oil, for cooking

For perfect sushi rice:
570 g (1 lb 4 oz/3 cups) short
 grain brown rice
1.9 l (64 fl oz/7½ cups) water
60 ml (2 fl oz/¼ cup) rice vinegar

To build the sushi:
10 roasted nori sheets
20 leaves romaine lettuce
1 medium cucumber, sliced
 into 20 slices
1-2 avocados, sliced into 20 slices
tamari, pickled ginger and
 Miso Mayo (page 115) to serve

Who doesn't love sushi? It's ever so versatile and infinitely delicious. This version pairs the decadence of sesame-crusted mushrooms with the fresh crunch of lettuce, cucumber and avocado. You can prep everything ahead of time and take turns rolling the sushi whilst enjoying Cucumber Sake-tinis (page 151) with friends. Invariably, some rolls will fall apart and mess will be made, but it's a delicious and fun way to spend an evening together.

For the Sesame-Crusted Mushrooms: Slice the mushrooms into 1 cm (½ in) wide slices, removing any long stalks if using shiitake. In a bowl, whisk together the flours, baking powder, salt and water to form a batter. Lightly grind the sesame seeds in mortar and pestle and then pour into a wide shallow bowl or dish.

Heat 3 tablespoons oil in a frying pan (skillet) over a medium–high heat. Coat the mushroom slices in the batter, wiping any excess on the edge of the bowl. Dip them into the sesame seeds to coat, then carefully place in the pan. Fry for 3 minutes on each side, then remove with a slotted spoon to drain on paper towels.

To make perfect sushi rice without a rice cooker: Place the rice and water in a medium-large saucepan and cover with a lid. Bring to the boil, then turn the heat down to the lowest heat possible. Leave the lid on the rice and allow to cook for 40 minutes. Turn off the heat and stir in the rice vinegar. Allow to stand with the lid on for another 10 minutes, then remove the lid and allow to cool. It's that simple!

To assemble: Dampen a sushi mat and place a sheet of nori on it. Spread about 3 heaped tablespoons of rice across the nori, using wet fingertips or the back of the spoon to flatten it and leaving about 3 cm (1 inch) of empty space at the top of the sheet. Top with 2 lettuce leaves, 2 mushroom slices, 2 slices of cucumber and 2 slices of avocado. Roll by lifting the mat and tucking the sushi up and over itself, to form a tight roll. Place seamside down on a wooden board and repeat with the remaining ingredients. Cut each roll into 8 slices with a wet serrated knife.

A very naughty and delicious thing you can do with this is to stir some miso mayo into the rice before rolling.

Note: Hate sushi or just can't be bothered rolling? This combination of ingredients also make incredible lettuce cups. Prepare everything as suggested and, instead of rolling into sushi rolls, place a little of each ingredient into a lettuce leaf and eat.

Pumpkin Pizza

If you've been to one of my supper clubs, chances are you've tried this pizza. I created the recipe years ago and the toppings evolved over time, until I landed on this version and never looked back. This recipe is definitely one for days when you are in a cooking mood, or have friends and family on hand to help out. Alternatively, you can use store-bought pesto and cashew-based cheese if you want to serve this for dinner but don't have time to make everything from scratch.

You can top the pizzas with anything you like and, of course, it can be fun to set up a pizza bar with everyone's favourite toppings. Here I've given my absolute favourite combo of all time, but feel free to top them with whatever your heart desires.

Makes 6 x 18 cm (7 in) diameter pizzas

Shopping list
For the base:
oil, for greasing
1 medium Hokkaido pumpkin or butternut squash (about 1 kg/2 lb 3 oz)
4 tablespoons psyllium husk
2 teaspoons baking powder
1 teaspoon salt
100 g (3½ oz/1 cup) almond flour
120 g (4 oz/1 cup) buckwheat flour

For the topping:
Green Pea Pesto, smooth version (page 48)
slow-roasted cherry tomatoes (see Note)
Kalamata olives, pitted and halved
Cashew Ricotta (page 124)

To serve:
rocket (arugula)
fresh basil leaves
olive oil

Preheat the oven to 190°C (375°F/Gas 5). Lightly oil a couple of baking trays (sheets).

Cut the pumpkin or squash in half, scrape out the seeds, and then cut each half into cubes, removing the skin as you go (if not using Hokkaido, aka the best pumpkin ever). Place the cubes in a medium saucepan and cover with water. Bring to the boil, then lower to a simmer and cook until the cubes are easily pierced with a fork, about 20 minutes. Drain, then use a fork to mash the pumpkin until smooth but still a little chunky.

Measure out about 500 g (1 lb 2 oz/2 cups) of mashed pumpkin. A little more or less is ok, but if you have a lot more save it for sandwiches, smoothies, hummus, or to make extra pizza bases (it's a pretty easy recipe to scale up). Combine the mash with the remaining base ingredients, stir to combine and then set aside for 5 minutes, while the psyllium works its magic. Divide the dough into 6 balls, press flat and then work into a circular shape with your fingertips. Place on the lightly oiled baking trays and cook in the hot oven for 15 minutes.

Remove from the oven, top with the pesto, tomatoes, olives and Cashew Ricotta and return to the oven for another 15 minutes. Allow to cool slightly before garnishing with rocket (arugula), basil leaves and a drizzle of olive oil. Enjoy immediately.

Note: To slow roast your own tomatoes, preheat the oven to 140°C (275°F/Gas 1). Lightly oil a baking tray (sheet). Slice the tomatoes in half and place on the tray, cut-side up. Sprinkle with a pinch of salt and a pinch of sugar, then roast in the oven for 2–3 hours.

Crumbed Chickpea Burgers

Serves 8

Shopping list
For the chickpea patties:
2 × 400 g (14 oz) tins chickpeas
  (garbanzo beans), drained and
  liquid reserved in a shallow dish
200 g (7 oz/1 cup) brown rice,
  cooked (to obtain 3 cups)
65 g (2¼ oz/½ cup) chickpea
  (gram) flour
1 tablespoon onion powder
1 tablespoon garlic powder
1 tablespoon smoked paprika
1 tablespoon maple syrup
1 teaspoon salt
10 g (½ oz/¼ cup) chopped
  coriander (cilantro) leaves
10 g (½ oz/½ cup) cornflakes
125 ml (4 fl oz/½ cup) canola oil,
  for cooking

To build and serve:
8 burger buns
Garlic Mayo (page 115)
Almond Butter Satay Sauce
  (page 120)
Pink Pickled Onions (page 116)
lettuce and cucumber
Smashed Potatoes (page 106)
Simple Green Salad (pg 108)
  (optional)

These burgers are next-level delicious. This is the closest I have ever come to deep frying something, which makes this the naughtiest dish in my repertoire. For that reason, I always cook double the rice for these burgers, as it's always nice to follow a decadent meal like this with a light meal of rice and steamed veggies, or simple sushi.

I've written this recipe with a crowd in mind, but you can easily halve it if you are just cooking for a small family.

Rinse the drained chickpeas well, place in a large bowl and mash until most of the chickpeas are broken down but some whole ones remain. Add the cooked rice, mash a few times to combine, then add the chickpea flour, spices, maple syrup and salt and stir until well combined. Finally, add the chopped coriander (cilantro) and stir until well combined. Place in the refrigerator for 30 minutes.

Meanwhile, use your hands or a mortar and pestle to crush the cornflakes and place them in a shallow dish. Remove the chickpea mixture from the refrigerator and form into 8 evenly sized balls. Flatten into patties, then dip first into the reserved chickpea liquid, then into the cornflake crumbs to coat.

Heat half the oil in a frying pan (skillet) over a medium heat. Fry 3–4 patties at a time until golden brown, about 5 minutes on each side, and then transfer on to paper towels to drain. Repeat with the remaining oil and patties.

Meanwhile, lightly toast the burger buns. Build the burgers by smearing garlic mayo on the bottom bun, then top with lettuce, a cooked patty, cucumber, pink pickled onions, almond butter satay sauce and finally the top bun. Enjoy with smashed potatoes.

Note: This recipe also makes amazing nuggets, which are wildly popular amongst the kids in my gang. You can get 3–4 smaller nuggets for each burger patty, so, depending on your kid-to-adult ratio, prepare the mixture accordingly. I usually skip the coriander (cilantro) and cornflake crumbs when making nuggets, and cook them for about 3 minutes on each side.

There's no shame in picking up chip-shop fries to serve with this burger, especially if it's a hot day and you don't want to turn on your oven.

Summer Rolls

Makes 12 rolls

Shopping list
For the filling:
400 g (14 oz) packet tofu,
   drained and pressed
200 g (7 oz) packet of rice noodles
½ × 340 g (11¾ oz) packet
   22 cm (8½ in) rice paper rolls
   (you won't need the whole packet)
fresh herbs, such as Vietnamese
   mint, Thai basil, coriander
   (cilantro) leaves
1 cucumber, thinly sliced
½ head red cabbage, thinly sliced
½ head lettuce, thinly sliced
1 or 2 avocados, thinly sliced
a few radishes, thinly sliced
1 red (bell) pepper, thinly sliced
1 just ripe mango, thinly sliced
2 carrots, very thinly sliced
black and white sesame seeds,
   lightly toasted

For the tofu marinade:
2 tablespoons tamari
2 tablespoons sriracha sauce
2 tablespoons mirin
2 tablespoons rice vinegar
1 tablespoon maple syrup
1 teaspoon grated fresh ginger

For the dipping sauce:
Almond Butter Satay Sauce
   (page 120) or for a lighter sauce:
60 ml (2 fl oz/¼ cup) rice vinegar
2 tablespoons soy sauce
2 tablespoons maple syrup
½ teaspoon tamarind paste

One of my favourite things to prepare when it's too hot to cook, nothing says summer like summer rolls. I usually get all the fillings and sauces ready before my guests arrive, then we sit down together and build them, stuffing ourselves silly with as many oddly shaped rolls as our bellies can accommodate. It's messy, fun and, most importantly, delicious.

The most important thing to know about making summer rolls, is that you only need to dunk the rice paper in the water for a short moment. It will still be hard, but will soften on your plate as you top it with ingredients and be soft enough to roll by the time you are ready to roll it. If you let it get too soft in the water, it becomes incredibly difficult to work with.

The second most important thing is that you should start with something flat, such as herbs or rounds of cucumber, as pointy things can make holes in your rice paper once you try to roll it.

The third most important thing is that, as with burritos, dumplings, sushi and all other foods where you are stuffing fillings into a wrapper, less is more when making these.

Thinly slice the tofu and place in a shallow dish. Combine the tofu marinade ingredients and pour over the tofu. Set aside in the refrigerator to marinate for at least 30 minutes or until feast time.

Cook the rice noodles according to the packet instructions. Have a small bowl of water on hand. Quickly dip your rice paper sheets into the water then lay them flat on your plate. Place your favourite fillings in the middle section of the wet rice paper, as pictured. I like to drizzle sauce over the top of my fillings before I roll, but you can also just serve the sauce for dipping, as you like. Once you've got all your fillings on the rice paper, fold up the bottom, then fold in the sides, then roll up tightly. Don't worry if your rolls aren't perfect – it takes practice! Mine are always tidy little packages but I manage to make a hell of a mess when eating them. Andy's usually resemble cigars more than summer rolls, but he manages to wolf them down without spilling a drop on his plate. Go figure!

If you want to make these to take to a potluck or picnic, cover with a damp tea towel to keep them fresh.

Miso Noodle Wonder Bowls

Reminiscent of ramen, these bowls were inspired by the trend that swept the food world a couple of years ago and seems as if it's here to stay. I love a light broth and noodle soup, especially when hungover, suffering from morning sickness, or craving something light but warming and filling. This recipe never fails to hit the spot.

Here, I share my basic broth recipe that you can enjoy year round, using the toppings I have suggested or whatever you are craving.

Serves 6

Shopping list
For the broth:
2 litres (68 fl oz/8 cups) water
1 piece of dried kombu/kelp
  (about 20 g/¾ oz)
20 g (¾ oz) dried shiitake
  mushrooms, sliced
thumb-sized piece fresh
  ginger, halved
½ onion, peeled and halved
1 carrot, peeled and halved
  lengthways
1 celery stalk (including leaves),
  cut into 4 pieces
60 ml (2 fl oz/¼ cup) tamari
60 ml (2 fl oz/¼ cup) mirin
100 g (3½ oz/3 heaped
  tablespoons) organic miso paste

For the toppings:
540 g (1 lb 3 oz) ramen noodles
  (see Note), cooked according
  to packet directions
carrot reserved from the broth,
  sliced into half-moons
Marinated Tofu (page 57 or
  store-bought), baked or quickly
  pan-seared
tenderstem broccoli (broccolini),
  pan-seared in a splash of broth
enoki mushrooms, pan-seared
  in a splash of broth
kimchi

For the broth: Fill a large saucepan or stockpot with the water. Add the kombu and dried shiitake and leave to soak for at least 1 hour.

Set the pan over a high heat, grate about 1 teaspoon of the ginger directly into the broth, then add the rest in chunks, along with the onion, carrot and celery. Bring the broth to the boil, then reduce the heat and simmer for 30 minutes. Add the tamari and mirin and simmer for another 15 minutes, then remove from the heat. Use tongs to remove and discard the kombu, onion, celery and ginger. Remove and reserve the carrot and, when cool enough to handle, cut into half-moons and set aside as a topping. Remove half a cup of the broth and stir in the miso paste until fully incorporated. Add the miso mixture back into the pan and stir to combine.

Enjoy immediately or set the broth aside until later. When you are ready to serve, reheat gently and don't bring to the boil or this will kill the precious probiotics in the miso.

To assemble: Arrange the cooked noodles in your serving bowls. Give the broth a good stir and pour 2 ladlefuls over the noodles. Top with your desired toppings, garnishes and condiments. Have fun experimenting with different combinations and enjoy!

Garnishes:
finely sliced spring onions
  (scallions)
coriander (cilantro) leaves
sesame seeds

Condiments:
sriracha sauce for spiciness
sesame oil for richness
rice vinegar or fresh lime juice
  for tanginess
maple syrup for sweetness

Note: You need about 90 g (3 ¼ oz) noodles per person. You can use any noodles you like, however true ramen noodles contain a special alkaline solution – kansui – which is what gives ramen noodles their signature yellowish colour, springy texture and prevents them from going mushy. I highly recommend using them, unless you are sensitive to gluten, in which case choose rice noodles, or soba noodles – if you can find some that are made without wheat flour (this can be tricky).

Curried Pumpkin Hummus
(page 40)

Pink Pickled Kohlrabi
(page 116)

Yoghurt Tahini Sauce
(page 120)

Miso Roasted Aubergines
(page 105)

Roast Veg Salad
(page 109)
with Tofu Feta
(page 124)

Veggie Balls
(page 84)

Beetroot &
Horseradish
Hummus
(page 40)

Veggie Balls

These balls are staples in our home and much-loved by all of my friends – kids and adults alike. Small children enjoy holding the ball and nibbling away at it, toddlers like to dunk them in sauce and adults can pop them in a wrap, on top of a salad, in a lettuce cup, or however their hearts desire. They are a great thing to make if you are hosting a potluck – ask your friends to bring salads, dips, pickles and breads to accompany them.

Preheat the oven to 200°C (400°F/Gas 6). Line a baking tray (sheet) with baking paper.

Place the grated veggies in a food processor and pulse a few times so that they become broken down but still chunky – you don't want to purée them. Add the peas and remaining ingredients and pulse until well combined, then transfer to a bowl and mix with your hands a few times to ensure everything is evenly combined. Roll into golfball-ish sized balls, placing on the lined baking tray as you go. Once all the balls are rolled, place them in the hot oven for 30 minutes, rotating each ball about 15 minutes into the cooking time.

I've served them with wraps, Roast Veg Salad (page 109), Tofu Feta (page 124), Beetroot & Horseradish Hummus (page 40), Pink Pickled Kohlrabi (page 116), pickles, olives, Miso-Roasted Aubergine (page 105) and Yoghurt Tahini Sauce (page 120). They are also incredible on top of any of the salads on pages 108–109, or shaped into veggie burgers or nuggets instead of balls.

Makes 15-20 balls
(I can eat 3-4 in one sitting
depending on hunger level and
what I'm serving them with)

Shopping list
135 g (4½ oz/1 cup) grated
 beetroot (beet)
135 g (4½ oz/1 cup) grated carrot
135 g (4½ oz/1 cup) grated
 sweet potato
125 g (4 oz/1 cup) frozen peas
125 g (4 oz/1 cup) chickpea
 (gram) flour
½ teaspoon ground turmeric
1 teaspoon ground coriander
1 teaspoon onion powder
1 teaspoon garlic powder
1 tablespoon cumin seeds
1 tablespoon sesame seeds
1 tablespoon maple or
 agave syrup
1 tablespoon olive or canola oil

Bowl Food

The bowl-food trend is sweeping the western food scene and with good reason. With so many people leading busy lives these days, cooking a nutritious meal from scratch every night of the week just isn't a reality. Bowl food allows you to do a bunch of prep when time allows, then build your dinner with ease before hanger kicks in. It's also a great way to feed groups and families with different tastes and picky little eaters. Everyone can add the ingredients they love and leave out the ones they don't. There are entire books dedicated to bowl food, so this recipe only scratches the surface of what's possible, but I wanted to give you some suggestions of bowls you can make, using some of the recipes in this book.

In addition to this, bowl food makes for an excellent potluck theme. Instead of everyone bringing mismatched - albeit delicious - dishes, you plan together what you are going to bring: a salad, a side, a pickle or a condiment, so that they all come together in perfect harmony to create lots of individually tailored feasts in bowls. Some examples:

Crumbed Cauliflower (page 64) / Miso-Roasted Aubergine (page 105) / Chopped Greek Salad (page 108) / Pink Pickled Onions (page 116)

Veggie Balls (left) / Roasted Carrots with Tahini & Maple (page 107) / Grain Salad (page 109) / Hummus (page 40)

Crumbed Chickpea Nuggets (page 76) / Za'atar-Crusted Green Beans (page 107) / Massaged Kale Chopped Salad (page 108) / Spicy Pepper Dip (page 38)

Pumpkin & Black Bean Rollups (page 46) / Simple Green Salad (page 108)/ Grilled Corn (page 54) / Quick Pickled Jalapeños (page 116) / Chipolte Cashew Cream (page 120)

Sushi Bowl - make all the Sesame Mushroom Sushi components (page 72) along with the Miso-Roasted Aubergine (Eggplant) (page 105) and serve them in a bowl instead

So, you are hosting a dinner party but you either can't - or don't want to - be cooking all day before your guests come over. Maybe it's a work night; maybe it's Christmas and you've got to be at family things all day before meeting your friends in the evening; maybe you'd rather be enjoying cocktails on your balcony while dinner sorts itself out in the kitchen. Whatever it is, I've got you. These dishes can all be prepared a day or two ahead of time and will taste better for it. Ask your friends to bring sides and salads, or perhaps a dip or nibbly thing to start with, and you've got yourself a right royal feast!

Planning Ahead

One-Pot Black Bean & Lentil Chilli

This hearty one-pot chilli is an easy way to feed a crowd with minimal mess. You can make it a day ahead of time if you need to be über-prepared and it also freezes well if you want to enjoy some now and the rest later.

Rinse the black beans and look over them for any stones. Soak overnight or during the day, then drain, but not fully as the black sediment at the bottom of the pot is what gives this chilli its incredible flavour. If you don't have time to soak or you simply forgot, don't worry! Black beans can be cooked from scratch without soaking (see the method in my Black Bean & Crumbled Cauliflower Tacos recipe (pages 64–65) as a guide). Place in a large saucepan with 1.4 litres (48 fl oz/6 cups) water, bring to the boil then add salt and lower to a simmer. Cook until you can easily squish a few beans on the side of the pot, this can be between 40 minutes and 2 hours, depending on the age of the beans and whether you soaked them. Keep the water level topped up during the cooking time, adding enough boiling water so that the beans are always covered by about 2 cm (¾ in).

Once the beans are soft, add the lentils, tomatoes, onions, mushrooms, garlic, coriander (cilantro), red (bell) pepper, courgette (zucchini), tomato paste and mushroom or bouillon powder. Increase the heat a little and cook for another 30 minutes, stirring frequently, until the lentils are soft and the veggies are cooked. Add the spinach and cook for another 2 minutes, then remove from the heat and cover with a lid until ready to serve.

It's rare that we eat this the same way twice. You can either enjoy this chilli on its own or pick something filling and starchy to ladle it onto. Andy's favourite way to eat it is on top of corn chips, but it's also soooo good on top of baked potatoes and incredible with a grain or cauliflower rice. Top with lots of yummy garnishes such as the ones suggested or anything else you have on hand. Enjoy!

Serves 6–8

Shopping list
For the stew:
300 g (10½ oz/1½ cups) dried black beans
1 teaspoon salt
300 g (10½ oz/1½ cups) dried beluga (black) lentils
2 × 400 g (14 oz) tins chopped tomatoes
2 yellow onions, finely chopped
500 g (1 lb 2 oz) assorted mushrooms, roughly chopped
4 garlic cloves, peeled and finely chopped
20 g (¾ oz/½ cup) coriander (cilantro), leaves and stalks, finely chopped
1 large red (bell) pepper, finely chopped
1 courgette (zucchini), finely chopped
2 tablespoons tomato paste
2 tablespoons Magical Mushroom Powder (page 122) or vegetable bouillon
200 g (7 oz) spinach, chopped

To serve:
cooked grains, cauliflower rice, baked potatoes or corn chips
vegan sour cream or Chipotle Cashew Cream (page 120)
Pink Pickled Onions (page 116)
sliced fresh or dried ground chillies
tinned or grilled sweetcorn
diced avocado
additional chopped coriander (cilantro) leaves
fresh lime, to squeeze

Great Shepherd's Pie

When you're in need of a veggie fix, look no further than this incredible pie that was shared with me by my friend Josh, who gave it this funny name because he grates the fillings, which gives this dish its surprising texture. Great for when you want something hearty and filling without the fartiness of pulses, or when you need a warm dish for Thanksgiving and Christmas-style feasts, that can complement pretty much any other dish.

Serves 4–8

Shopping list
For the topping:
1 kg (2 lb 3 oz) potatoes, peeled
  and cut into chunks
sea salt to taste, plus ½ teaspoon
2 tablespoons coconut oil
½ teaspoon ground nutmeg
60–125 ml (2–4 fl oz/¼–½ cup)
  plant-based milk
3–4 tablespoons Walnut Sprinkles
  (page 122), to garnish

For the filling:
1 large aubergine (eggplant),
  cut into 1 cm (½ in) chunks
1 teaspoon salt
2 tablespoons olive oil
1 large onion, finely chopped
handful of mushrooms (about
  250 g/9 oz), grated
1 large courgette (zucchini), grated
1 large carrot, grated
1 large beetroot (beet), grated
2 garlic cloves, finely chopped
1 tablespoon tomato paste
1 tablespoon vegan
  Worcestershire sauce (optional)
1 teaspoon dried thyme
salt and freshly ground black
  pepper to taste

Place the potatoes in a large saucepan of salted water. Bring to the boil, then lower to a simmer and cook for 20–30 minutes. Drain and allow to cool for 10 minutes, then mash with the coconut oil, ½ teaspoon sea salt, nutmeg and enough milk to obtain a smooth, but not runny, mash. Set aside.

Meanwhile, place the aubergine in a colander, sprinkle with 1 teaspoon salt, toss and set aside to drain.

Place the oil in a large frying pan (skillet) over a medium heat. Add the onion and cook until translucent, about 5 minutes. Add the drained aubergine to the pan and cook until it starts to soften, about 10–15 minutes. Add the mushrooms and courgette and cook, stirring frequently, until reduced by about half, about 20 minutes. Add the carrot, beetroot, garlic, tomato paste, Worcestershire sauce, thyme, and salt and pepper to taste, and cook for another 10 minutes. Transfer to an ovenproof dish.

Top the filling with the mash, then run over the surface of the mash with the tines of a fork. Scatter the walnut sprinkles over, then set aside until ready to cook. Cover with a clean tea towel if you aren't planning on doing this in the next few hours. Pop in the refrigerator if planning on cooking the next day and remove about 30 minutes before you plan to put it in the oven.

When ready to cook, preheat the oven to 190°C (375°F/Gas 5). Bake the pie in the hot oven for 20 minutes. Remove and devour, either alone or with an array of sides. Yum. (See photo overleaf.)

Whole Cauliflower Tadka

Growing up, I never ate cauliflower because my mum despised it. She was scarred from the cauliflower of her own childhood, and I always thought I hated it too until I was well into my twenties and the cauliflower revolution was in full swing. These days, it's one of the most wildly popular vegetables out there, due to its malleability in both flavour and texture. In this recipe I keep the cauliflower whole, making it one of those dishes that makes everyone say 'wow!' excitedly when I present it at the table. Whilst the flavours are Indian-inspired, it goes with pretty much anything and it can be served as a main or as a side.

Melt the coconut oil in an ovenproof pan over a medium–high heat. Add the onion and cook until translucent, about 5 minutes. Add the tomato, asafoetida and and curry powder and cook, stirring, for 2 minutes, then add the lentils, garlic and black salt, plus 500 ml (17 fl oz/2 cups) water. Cover, bring to the boil, then lower to a simmer for 20 minutes.

Preheat oven to 200°C (400°F/Gas 6). Add the coconut milk to the lentils along with 200 ml (7 fl oz/generous ¾ cup) water and stir to combine. Remove the tough outer leaves from the cauliflower and cut off the stalk so that it's flat-bottomed. Use a small paring knife to cut a deep cross into the bottom of the stalk and then gently place the cauliflower into the curry. Cover with a tight-fitting lid or foil and place in the hot oven for 1 hour.

Remove from the oven and allow to rest, covered, for 10 minutes before carefully removing the lid/foil.

To make the tadka: Melt the coconut oil in a large frying pan (skillet) over a medium-high heat. Add the cumin and mustard seeds and stir constantly until they start to pop. Add the turmeric and hing and stir for about 30 seconds, then pour the tadka over the cooked cauliflower.

Sprinkle with finely chopped parsley or coriander (cilantro) before serving. To serve, cut the cauliflower into slices like a piece of cake and place in a bowl, then ladle some of the lentil curry over the top. If you've never made this before you might feel inclined to serve it with rice, but you really don't need it as the cauliflower acts like rice, soaking up the curry and giving the dish the texture that rice would usually lend. (See photo overleaf.)

Serves 4–8

Shopping list

1 tablespoon coconut oil
1 medium onion, finely chopped
1 large tomato, finely chopped
pinch of asafoetida (hing)
3 tablespoons curry powder
100 g (3½ oz/½ cup) beluga
   (black) lentils
3–5 garlic cloves, finely chopped
1 teaspoon black salt
600 ml (20 fl oz/2½ cups)
   coconut milk
1 head cauliflower (about 900 g/
   2 lb, or about 18 cm (7 in)
   in diameter)
large handful of parsley or
   coriander (cilantro) leaves,
   finely chopped, to garnish

For the tadka:

2 tablespoons coconut oil
1 teaspoon cumin seeds
1 teaspoon mustard seeds
½ teaspoon ground turmeric
¼ teaspoon asafoetida (hing)

Great
Shepherd's Pie
(page 90)

Smashed
Potatoes
(page106)

Simple
Green Salad
(page 108)

Whole
Cauliflower
Tadka
(page 91)

Maultaschen
(page 95)

Hasselback
Butternut
(page 104)

Maultaschen

Maultaschen are the giant, German cousins of ravioli. They are delicious as a main, or as a starter when having a multi-course feast. They store well in the refrigerator or freezer, which makes them a perfect thing to prepare ahead of time.

Makes 12 giant dumplings
Serves 6-12 as a starter
or 3-4 as a main

Shopping list
For the filling:
2 tablespoons olive oil
2 shallots, finely chopped
200 g (7 oz) brown mushrooms,
   finely chopped
60 g (2 oz/½ cup) tightly packed
   sauerkraut, squeezed and juice
   retained for the soup broth
   (see below)
125 ml (4 fl oz/½ cup) white wine
1 teaspoon sea salt
½ teaspoon dried thyme
¼ teaspoon ground nutmeg
¼ teaspoon freshly ground
   black pepper
1 heaped tablespoon plain
   (all-purpose) flour

For the dough:
260 g (9½ oz/2 cups) plain
   (all-purpose) flour, plus extra
   for dusting
1 teaspoon salt
180 ml (6½ fl oz/¾ cup) warm water

For the soup broth:
1 tablespoon olive oil
1 small white onion, sliced into rings
2 small carrots, sliced
2 stalks celery, sliced
1 litre (34 fl oz/4 cups)
   vegetable stock
60 ml (2 fl oz/¼ cup) white wine
2 tablespoons sauerkraut juice
   (or whatever you obtained
   from squeezing the sauerkraut
   in the filling)
30 g (1 oz/¼ cup) frozen peas
fresh chives to garnish

For the filling: Place the olive oil in a large frying pan (skillet) over a medium heat. Add the shallots and cook until translucent, about 5 minutes. Add the mushrooms and cook until soft, about 10 minutes. Add the sauerkraut, along with the white wine, salt, thyme, nutmeg and black pepper. Cook until the wine has almost evaporated, then sprinkle the flour over. The mixture should thicken significantly. Cook for another 5 minutes, stirring constantly, then remove from heat and allow to cool while you prepare the dough.

For the dough: Combine the flour and salt in a large mixing bowl. Add the warm water and knead into a smooth dough. Separate into 2 balls and set aside, covered with a tea towel, for 10-15 minutes, while you prepare the broth ingredients.

On a lightly floured surface, flatten the first ball of dough, fold into a rectangle and then roll into a long rectangle about 60 cm (24 in) long and 20 cm (8 in) wide. Place 6 neat tablespoons of filling along the length of the dough, about a thumb's width apart. Wet the gaps between the filling, then fold the dough over from each side to enclose the filling, wetting the underside of the edge that will become the top seam. Cut into 6 dumplings, then crimp the cut edges with a fork, folding up the sides on the very outer edges if you need to, to prevent the filling falling out. Repeat with remaining dough.

For the broth: Place the olive oil in a large saucepan over a medium heat. Add the onions and cook for 2 minutes. Add the carrots and celery, cook for another 2 minutes, then add the vegetable stock, wine and sauerkraut juice and bring to the boil. Add the peas and the *maultaschen* dumplings, 6 at a time, and cook until they float to the surface, about 10 minutes. Place in serving bowls and, once all of the *maultaschen* are cooked, ladle the broth over them. Serve garnished with chives or whatever other fresh herbs you have on hand.

One-Pot Spaghetti with Aubergine Balls

Spaghetti, oh spaghetti. Popular with people of all ages, this dish is one of my favourite things to cook when we have friends with children coming for dinner. I've written this one with a feast in mind, hence the addition of the aubergine (eggplant) balls and the suggestion to serve with bread and salad, but the one-pot spaghetti is also a great one to make for a quick weeknight dinner.

I usually prep the balls ahead of time and then pop them in the oven when I start making the sauce, so that I can have my kitchen as clean as possible before guests arrive. They freeze well too, so you can always have a batch in the freezer and then throw together a delicious feast for an impromptu dinner.

Serves 4-8

Shopping list
For the aubergine (eggplant) balls:
2 tablespoons olive oil
2-3 shallots, finely diced
2 large aubergines (eggplant), finely diced
up to 250 ml (8½ fl oz/1 cup) water
3 garlic cloves, peeled and finely diced
zest and juice of 1 lemon
6 sun-dried tomatoes, finely diced
1 tablespoon balsamic vinegar
½ teaspoon dried rosemary
½ teaspoon dried oregano
1 teaspoon salt
50 g (2 oz/1 cup) breadcrumbs (see Note)

For the one-pot spaghetti:
2 tablespoons olive oil
1 medium brown onion, finely diced
350 g (12 oz) cherry tomatoes, halved
2 x 400 g (14 oz) tins chopped tomatoes
1 bay leaf
3 garlic cloves, peeled
125 ml (4 fl oz/½ cup) red wine
1 tablespoon tomato paste
2 tablespoons capers (optional)
1 teaspoon sugar
1 teaspoon sea salt
500 g (1 lb 2 oz) packet wholewheat spaghetti (see Note)

To serve:
Walnut Sprinkles (page 122)
fresh basil leaves
fresh bread
Simple Green Salad (page 108)

To make the balls: Place the oil in a large frying pan (skillet) over a medium heat. Add the shallots and cook until translucent, about 5 minutes. Add the aubergine and cook until soft, about 15–20 minutes, adding water as you go to stop it from sticking to the bottom of the pan. When the aubergine is all soft and mushy, add the garlic, lemon, sun-dried tomatoes, vinegar, herbs and salt. Stir for 2 minutes, then add the breadcrumbs and remove from the heat. Stir well, adding more water if necessary so that all of the breadcrumbs are wet and the mixture holds together well. Allow to cool.

Meanwhile, preheat the oven to 180°C (350°F/Gas 4) and line a baking tray (sheet) with baking paper. Roll tablespoons of mixture into balls and place on the lined baking tray. Bake in the hot oven for 30 minutes.

For the sauce: Place the oil in a large saucepan over a medium heat. Add the onions and cook until translucent, about 5 minutes. Add the tomatoes and use a potato masher to break them up a little. Add the remaining ingredients, except the spaghetti, and simmer for 10 minutes.

When you are ready to add the spaghetti, add 1 litre (34 fl oz/4 cups) water to the pan and bring to the boil. Break the spaghetti noodles in half and add to the sauce. Yes, to the sauce. Cover and bring back to the boil, then remove the lid, lower the heat, and allow to cook for 10 minutes, gently stirring a couple of times during the cooking time. Remove from the heat and allow to stand for 5–10 minutes. It will thicken significantly during this time.

Spoon the spaghetti into bowls, top with the balls, walnut sprinkles and fresh basil leaves. Serve with a simple side salad and warm crusty bread and you've got yourself a proper feast. (See photo overleaf.)

Note: Gluten-free folk! You can substitute the breadcrumbs for chickpea flour in the aubergine (eggplant) balls. You can use gluten-free pasta in place of wholewheat spaghetti or you can use courgetti (zoodles) – however, if using courgetti (zoodles), make the sauce as directed but skip the extra water and add the courgetti (zoodles) for the final 2–3 minutes of cooking time.

Butternut Lentil Lasagne

Comfort food at its finest, this dish is perfect for cosy nights in. It's filling, filled with nutrients and, like all lasagne, it gets better with time. Make it the night before you have guests coming for dinner, for a friend who has just had a baby, or for a friend who is unwell and needs a bit of extra nourishment.

To make the sauce: Place the oil in a medium saucepan over a medium heat. Add the onion and cook until translucent, about 5 minutes. Add the lentils and 500 ml (17 fl oz/2 cups) water, cover and cook for 15 minutes. Add the remaining sauce ingredients and simmer for another 30 minutes, by which point you should have a thick, decadent sauce.

Meanwhile, prepare the squash (cutting it into individual slices once cooked), green pea pesto and walnut sprinkles. Cook the lasagna sheets, if required.

Preheat the oven to 200°C (400°F/Gas 6).
In a large deep baking dish, build your lasagne in layers as follows:

1_ lasagne sheet / 2 ladlefuls of sauce
2_ lasagne sheet / squash / pesto
3_ lasagne sheet / 2 ladlefuls of sauce
4_ lasagne sheet / squash / pesto
5_ lasagne sheet / remaining sauce

Cover with foil and bake in the hot oven for 45 minutes. Remove the foil and cook for another 15 minutes so that the top can get all crispy and crunchy.

Allow to cool for 10 minutes before serving with a simple side salad, a generous scattering of Walnut Sprinkles and some fresh basil and parsley leaves.

Note: This is not a pretty dish when it comes out of the oven, but once its been cut and sprinkled with garnishes it looks great. If you are taking it to a friend's and want to present it well, sprinkle the Walnut Sprinkles and fresh herbs over it right before you deliver it. Alternatively, you can arrange halved cherry tomatoes or thin slices of tomato on top of the lentils, before you bake, if you want your lasagna to be a little easier on the eye.

Gluten-free folk can enjoy this with gluten-free pasta. Depending on where you live, you may not be able to find gluten-free lasagne sheets, but penne is pretty common and works great – you just have to cook it first and have the patience to line all the little penne up, one by one.

Serves 4-8

Shopping list:
1 butternut squash (about 1 kg/
   2 lb 3 oz), cooked hasselback-
   style as on page 104
Green Pea Pesto (page 48)
Walnut Sprinkles (page 122)
20 lasagne sheets
additional basil and parsley
   leaves to garnish

For the tomato and lentil sauce:
1 tablespoon olive oil
1 brown onion, finely chopped
200 g (7 oz/1 cup) beluga
   (black) lentils
2 × 400 g (14 oz) tins chopped
   tomatoes
½ teaspoon each dried rosemary,
   dried thyme, dried oregano
   and dried sage
1 teaspoon fennel seeds
1 teaspoon balsamic vinegar
1 tablespoon tomato paste
6 brown mushrooms
1 teaspoon salt

There's nothing better than a plate full of different flavours and textures. When cooking vegan food, vegetables are often the star of the show which means that sides and salads can be served as a complement to a 'main' meal or enjoyed as standalone meals in their own right. All of the recipes in the following chapter can be served together, and make great additions to many of the other recipes I've shared throughout this book. I hope your friends and family love these dishes as much as mine do. All of them have been served at the massive, boozy potluck dinners we used to host and attend in our childless Berlin years and have made it into this book because the are the things most often requested by friends or myself when we ask each other 'What should I bring..?'

Seven Sides

& Seven Salads

All sides serve 4–8

7

Sides

Everything you see here is cooked in a 190°C (375°F/Gas 5) oven, which makes making a few of them at once an absolute breeze. Pair with wintery classics such as Great Shepherd's Pie (page 90), or the nut roast from my first book and my blog, or with summery salads, and you have a light and nutritious meal.

1. Hasselback Butternut

Shopping list
1 large butternut squash
1 tablespoon olive oil, plus
    extra for greasing
1 tablespoon maple syrup
½ teaspoon fine sea salt
½ teaspoon dried thyme
3 garlic cloves, finely sliced
a few sprigs of rosemary
50 g (2 oz/½ cup) pecans,
    roughly chopped

Cut the butternut squash in half and scrape out the seeds. Remove the skin by standing up one half, holding it firmly and gently cutting away the skin with a small but strong vegetable knife. It's a bit of effort but well worth the outcome. Lay the squash cut-side down on a chopping board. Lay chopsticks or wooden spoons along either side, then cut deep grooves into the squash at 2–3 mm (⅛ in) intervals all the way along the length (the chopsticks will prevent you from cutting all the way through). Gently transfer to a lightly oiled baking tray. In a small bowl, combine the olive oil, maple syrup, sea salt and thyme and brush half of this over the butternut. Place in a hot oven for 15 minutes. Remove from the oven, then insert the garlic slices and sprigs of rosemary between the cut grooves, brush with the remaining marinade, sprinkle with chopped pecans and return to oven for a further 15 minutes.

2. Curry-Roasted Chickpeas

Shopping list
400 g (14 oz) tin chickpeas (garbanzo beans),
    drained, rinsed and dried with a tea towel
1 tablespoon olive oil
1 tablespoon curry powder
1 tablespoon nutritional yeast
1 teaspoon maple syrup
½ teaspoon sea salt

Place all the ingredients in a mixing bowl and use your hands to coat the chickpeas with the seasonings. Spread over a baking tray and place in the hot oven for 20 minutes for soft-roasted chickpeas; 30 minutes for crispy ones.

3. Miso-Roasted Aubergine

Shopping list
8 skinny or 3 large aubergines (eggplant)
1 tablespoon sea salt
1 heaped tablespoon miso paste
60 ml (2 fl oz/¼ cup) tamari
1 teaspoon grated fresh ginger
1 garlic clove, grated
2 tablespoons water

Cut each aubergine in half lengthways, sprinkle with the salt and set aside to sweat for 15–30 minutes. Combine all the remaining ingredients in a small bowl and set aside. Pat the aubergine dry with a clean tea towel and carefully score the flesh in a criss-cross pattern with a sharp knife. Lay on a baking tray (sheet) and brush with the marinade, jiggling the brush a little to get the marinade in between all those score lines. Place in the hot oven for 15 minutes. Remove from the oven, brush again with any remaining marinade and return to oven for another 15 minutes.

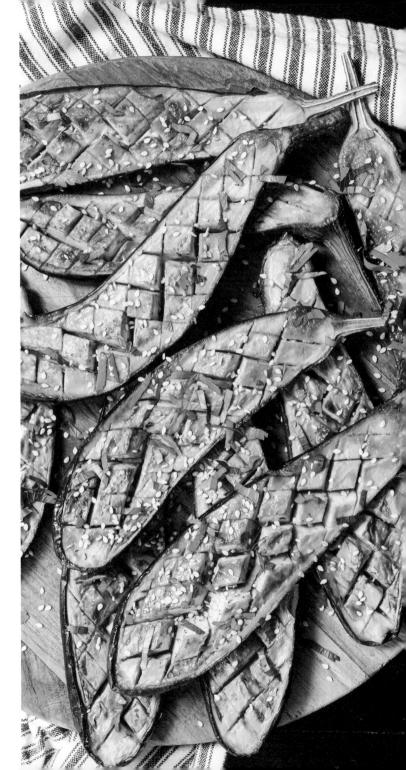

4. Smashed Potatoes

Shopping list
1 kg (2 lb 3 oz) baby potatoes,
  washed but skins left on
½ teaspoon sea salt, plus extra
  to salt the cooking water
2 tablespoons olive oil
fresh herbs, such as rosemary, thyme,
  coriander (cilantro) or chives
freshly ground black pepper

To serve:
Garlic Mayo (page 115)

Place the potatoes in a large saucepan of
salted water. Bring to the boil and cook for
10–15 minutes, until easily pierced with a
fork. Drain, allow to cool, then transfer to an
oiled baking tray (sheet). Lightly smash each
potato with a fork or potato masher. Don't do
it too hard – you want the potato to remain
whole, but you just want to break it a little so
that it has more surface area to get all crispy
and delicious. Brush with the oil, sprinkle with
salt and herbs (if using rosemary or thyme)
and place in the hot oven for 30 minutes.
Remove from the oven, sprinkle with herbs
(if using coriander or chives) and lots of
cracked pepper and serve with garlic mayo.

All sides serve 4–8

5. Za'atar-Crusted Green Beans

Shopping list
400 g (14 oz) green beans, trimmed
65 g (2¼ oz/½ cup) brown rice flour
125 ml (4 fl oz/½ cup) water
1 tablespoon olive oil
2 teaspoons sesame seeds
2 teaspoons dried thyme
2 teaspoons dried oregano
1 teaspoon sumac
½ teaspoon sea salt

Place the beans in a large saucepan of salted water. Bring to the boil and cook for 5 minutes, then drain and rinse with cold water. Spread onto a clean tea towel and allow to dry. In a large mixing bowl, whisk the rice flour and water into a batter, then toss the beans in the batter. Grease a baking tray (sheet) with the olive oil. Place the sesame seeds, herbs, sumac and salt in a mortar and pestle and lightly grind into the za'tar mixture. Place the battered beans on the tray, sprinkle with half the za'atar mixture, toss to coat, then sprinkle with remaining za'atar. Bake in the hot oven for 15 minutes.

6. Ginger & Garlic Mushrooms

Shopping list
10 large brown mushrooms
oil for greasing
thumb-sized piece fresh ginger, finely minced
4 garlic cloves, peeled and finely minced
2 tablespoons tamari
2 tablespoons sesame oil
chopped coriander (cilantro) leaves
   and white sesame seeds to garnish (optional)

Gently remove the stalks from the mushrooms and place, gills facing up, on a lightly oiled baking tray (sheet). In a small bowl, combine the rest of the ingredients into a marinade. Pop 1 teaspoon of the marinade into each mushroom cap. Cook in the hot oven for 30 minutes. Sprinkle with a little chopped coriander and sesame seeds before serving, as they are not the prettiest little fellas, but by god they are delicious.

7. Roasted Carrots with Tahini & Maple

Shopping list
1 kg (2 lb 3 oz) carrots, preferably
   with leafy tops still on
1 tablespoon olive oil
½ teaspoon sea salt
2 tablespoons maple syrup
60 ml (2 fl oz/¼ cup) tahini
large handful of pomegranate seeds

Break the leafy tops off the carrots, leaving 2–3 cm (1 in) of greenery still attached. Peel and cut any large ones in half lengthways then toss in the oil, salt and 1 tablespoon of the maple syrup. Spread onto a baking tray (sheet) and place in the hot oven for 30 minutes. In a small bowl, combine the tahini and maple syrup and a little water if necessary (this will depend on the thickness of the tahini you are using). Drizzle the tahini sauce over the carrots and top with pomegranate seeds.

All salads serve 4-8

7

Salads

Follow the same method for all the salads: Place the ingredients in a large bowl in the order listed. Toss or stir to combine, then add dressing directly before serving. They can all be eaten as mains, if wished.

1. Simple Green Salad

Shopping list
a few handfuls of any light leafy green, such as rocket (arugula), spinach or lettuce
1 bulb fennel, finely sliced
3 tomatoes, cut into chunks, or 10-15 cherry tomatoes, halved
1 cucumber, finely sliced or cut into chunks
1 avocado, cut into chunks
large handful of olives
large handful of toasted walnuts

Dressing:
Balsamic Reduction (page 121)

2. Chopped Greek Salad

Shopping list
1 head of lettuce, roughly chopped
1 green pepper, cut into 2 cm (¾ in) slices
5 large tomatoes, cut into 2 cm (¾ in) chunks
1 cucumber, cut into 2 cm (¾ in) chunks
1 red onion, finely sliced
large handful of olives
½ quantity Tofu Feta (page 124)
1 avocado, cut into 2 cm (¾ in) chunks (optional, not very traditional but so yummy)

Dressing:
60 ml (2 fl oz/¼ cup) olive oil
1 tablespoon red wine vinegar
¼ teaspoon dried oregano
¼ teaspoon sea salt

3. Massaged Kale Chopped Salad

Shopping list
225 g (8 oz/1½ cups) cooked chickpeas (garbanzo beans) (or a 400 g (14 oz) tin, drained and rinsed)
5 large kale leaves (tear into smaller pieces, sprinkle with ½ teaspoon fine sea salt and massage until limp)
2-3 stalks celery, finely chopped
3 large tomatoes, finely chopped
1 red onion, finely chopped
1 red (bell) pepper, finely chopped
1 avocado, finely chopped
handful of olives, finely chopped
large handful flaked or slivered almonds, toasted

Dressing:
plain lemon juice or Balsamic Reduction (page 121)
olive oil (optional)

Hot tip! To get the pits out of the olives, press down on them with the flat part of a large knife. The flesh will easily come away from the pit. Discard the pits and then do with the flesh as you wish.

4. Gnocchi Salad

Shopping list
400 g (14 oz) gnocchi, cooked
    according to packet instructions
200 g (7 oz) cherry tomatoes, halved
200 g (7 oz) Kalamata olives, halved
basil leaves, as many as possible
    (I usually use a small plant's worth)
sea salt and freshly cracked black
    pepper to taste

Dressing:
drizzle of olive oil
Balsamic Reduction (page 121)

5. Grain Salad

Shopping list
3 cups cooked cracked freekeh
250 g (9 oz/1½ cups) cooked lentils
    (or a 400 g (14 oz) tin, drained and rinsed)
1 red onion, finely chopped
large handful of parsley leaves, finely chopped
large handful of coriander (cilantro)
    leaves, finely chopped
handful of capers, finely chopped
handful of currants
1 large handful each pine nuts, sunflower
    seeds and slivered almonds, lightly toasted
1 tablespoon cumin seeds, lightly toasted
    (can toast with the nuts and seeds)
a generous sprinkling of pomegranate seeds

Dressing:
60 ml (2 fl oz/¼ cup) olive oil
60 ml (2 fl oz/¼ cup) apple cider vinegar
1 tablespoon maple syrup

6. Satay Noodle Salad

Shopping list
2 heads Romaine lettuce, thinly sliced
200 g (7 oz) rice or udon noodles, cooked
    according to packet instructions, then
    tossed in 125 ml (4 fl oz/½ cup)
    Almond Butter Satay Sauce (page 120)
2 large carrots, peeled and julienned
1 large cucumber, thinly sliced
½ red onion, finely diced
large handful of roasted peanuts
large handful of coriander (cilantro) leaves,
    finely chopped
juice of 1 lime
Tofu Skewers or Baked Tofu (page 57)

Dressing:
125 ml (4 fl oz/½ cup) Almond Butter Satay
    Sauce (page 120), drizzled over once served

7. Roast Veg Salad

Shopping list
100 g (3½ oz/2 cups) baby spinach
300 g (10½ oz/2 cups) cooked quinoa
300 g (10½ oz/2 cups) roasted
    chopped veggies, such as pumpkin,
    sweet potato, courgette (zucchini), etc.
large handful of chopped semi-dried tomatoes
large handful of whole roasted almonds
½ quantity Tofu Feta (page 124)
1 red onion, finely sliced
zest of 1 lemon

Dressing:
lemon juice
olive oil

Massaged
Kale Chopped
Salad
(page 108)

Gnocchi
Salad
(page 109)

Satay
Noodle Salad
(page 109)

Chopped
Greek Salad
(page 108)

Condiments

Condiments are renowned for their unparalleled ability to elevate a dish. From the big brand sauces that steal the hearts of nations, to the special recipe sauces and pickles that are unique to a family or region, they lend distinction to meals, both in flavour and identity.

Coming together in the heart of the home, condiments mingle with our souls, creating nostalgia and the ability to whip up a feast practically any time, with very little effort. Our refrigerator is always full of them and these are some of my homemade faves.

Sprinkles & Basics

Easy Mayo 3 Ways

Vegan mayo is pretty easy to find these days, but the cheap ones taste like crap and the good ones can be very pricey. Luckily, a tasty version is easy to make at home in just a couple of minutes and with just a few ingredients. It's fatty - it's basically emulsified vegetable oil that has been flavoured with sugar, salt and spices, but it's a treat, and a much healthier one than anything you'll find on a supermarket shelf.

Place everything in a high-speed blender and blitz until thick and creamy – about 30 seconds. Use immediately or transfer to an airtight jar and store in the fridge for up to 1 week.

*Makes about 400 ml
(13½ fl oz/1½ cups)*

Shopping list
For miso mayo:
250 ml (8½ fl oz/1 cup) canola oil
125 ml (4 fl oz/½ cup) soy milk
2 tablespoons sesame oil
2 tablespoons rice vinegar
2 tablespoons light miso paste
1 tablespoon maple syrup
2 teaspoons tamari
1 teaspoon wasabi powder

For sweet curried mayo:
250 ml (8½ fl oz/1 cup) canola oil
125 ml (4 fl oz/½ cup) soy milk
1 heaped tablespoon curry powder
2 tablespoons white wine vinegar
2 tablespoons maple syrup
1 teaspoon salt

For garlic mayo:
250 ml (8½ fl oz/1 cup) canola oil
125 ml (4 fl oz/½ cup) soy milk
2 tablespoons white wine vinegar
1 tablespoon maple syrup
1 teaspoon salt
2 teaspoons finely chopped garlic
   (about 2 cloves)

Quick Pickles

Quick pickles are an excellent way to get acquainted with preserving foods and they make a tangy and vibrant addition to any meal.

For a basic vinegar solution that will guarantee delicious pickles, use the following:

Vinegar	Sugar	Salt
125ml (4 fl oz/½ cup)	1 tablespoon	½ teaspoon
1 litre (34 fl oz/4 cups)	100 g (3½ oz/½ cup)	4 teaspoons

In addition to this you can add crushed garlic cloves and all kinds of spices, such as the ones suggested in the recipe below.

The amount of vinegar you will need depends on the size of your jar and how tightly you pack your veggies, but I find that a half-volume of the jar is usually a good amount. So, for a 500 ml (17 fl oz/2 cup) jar, use 250 ml (8½ fl oz/1 cup) vinegar. If it's not quite enough you can top it up with boiling water.

Place the vinegar, sugar and salt in a small saucepan over a medium-high heat. Stir frequently until the sugar and salt are dissolved. Meanwhile, crush the garlic (if using), and place in the sterilized jar along with any spices. Peel and chop veggies as suggested and tightly pack into the jar. Pour the hot vinegar solution into the jar and top up with boiling water, if necessary. Secure the lid, allow to cool and then transfer to the refrigerator or pantry until ready to use.

Shopping list
Quick Pickled Jalapeños:
(For a 250 ml/8½ fl oz/1 cup jar)
125 ml (4 fl oz/½ cup) white
   wine vinegar
1 tablespoon sugar
½ teaspoon sea salt
1 garlic clove, peeled and crushed
9-10 green jalapeños,
   cut into thin slices

Pink Pickled Kohlrabi:
(For a 500 ml/17 fl oz/2 cup jar)
250 ml (8½ fl oz/1 cup)
   white wine vinegar
2 tablespoons sugar
1 teaspoon salt
3 garlic cloves, peeled
1 teaspoon cumin seeds
1 teaspoon caraway seeds
½ small beetroot (beet),
   halved or quartered
1 kohlrabi, cut into 5 mm (¼ in)
   wide matchsticks

Pink Pickled Onions:
(For a 750 ml/25 fl oz/3 cup jar)
375 ml (12 fl oz/1½ cups)
   white wine vinegar
3 tablespoons sugar
1½ teaspoons salt
juice of 2 limes (add this
   to vinegar solution)
1 teaspoon coriander seeds
1 teaspoon black peppercorns
4 red onions, peeled and
   thinly sliced

Magical Mushroom Powder *(page 122)*

Cashew Ricotta *(page 124)*

Quick Pickled Jalapeños *(left)*

Tofu Feta *(page 124)*

Walnut Sprinkles *(page 122)*

Pink Pickled Onions *(left)*

Tofu Scramble Seasoning *(page 28)*

Storage: If you plan to store your pickles on the shelf for later consumption, first make sure to sterilize your jars and lids. Either wash them in warm soapy water, rinse and pop them in a 160°C (320°F/ Gas 3) oven for 15 minutes, or stand them in a large pan, cover with hot water, then boil for 15 minutes. Remember to boil the lids and, if using rubber seals, give them a dunk in the hot water too.

Onion Gravy for Sunday Roasts

This one is more of an idea than a recipe. A reminder, perhaps, that roasts can still be a thing even if you remove the meat. To me, the best thing about a Sunday roast is the gathering of friends in a cosy home with the fireplace roaring. As long as there are potatoes and gravy, I couldn't give a darn what else is served, and that's what makes the Sunday roast tradition so wonderful. If you want to try something new, there are plenty of recipes for sides and salads in the Seven Sides and Seven Salads chapter (pages 104–109), but it's just as common for us to chop up a bunch of different veggies, toss them in olive oil and salt, and pop them into a hot oven for half an hour. Slather them in this delicious onion gravy and enjoy your Sunday feast.

Melt the coconut oil in a medium saucepan over a medium heat. Add the onion and cook, stirring regularly, until soft and translucent, about 5 minutes. Add the garlic and cook for another minute, then add the flour, sugar, nutritional yeast, soy sauce and dried herbs, stirring until a smooth paste forms. Add the hot stock, little by little, whisking as you go to ensure no lumps form. Bring the mixture to the boil and keep whisking until the gravy thickens.

Allow to cool, then purée until smooth – either use a hand-held blender or transfer to a high-speed blender (I prefer the latter as this ensures the smoothest, silkiest consistency). Serve immediately, or prepare in advance and reheat when your roast veggies are ready.

Serves 4-8

Shopping list
3 tablespoons coconut oil
1 onion, finely chopped
3 garlic cloves, peeled and crushed
110 g (3 ¾ oz/generous ¾ cup)
   plain (all-purpose) flour
pinch sugar
2 tablespoons nutritional yeast
   (yeast flakes)
1 tablespoon soy sauce
1 teaspoon dried sage
1 teaspoon dried thyme
1 litre (35 fl oz/4 cups) hot
   vegetable stock

6

Sauces

A good sauce can make or break a dish. These are recipes that I've developed over the past few years that never fail to bring a meal together and go with the recipes in this book.

Chipotle Cashew Cream

Makes 250 ml (8½ fl oz/1 cup)

Shopping list
150 g (5 oz/1 cup) cashews
1 chipotle pepper in adobo sauce,
   or 1 tablespoon chipotle paste

Soak the cashews overnight or boil them in water for 15 minutes. Drain and rinse the nuts, then place in a high-speed blender. Add the pepper or paste and enough water so that the cashews are just covered. Blend until smooth, adding a little more water if necessary. Transfer to an airtight container and place in the refrigerator until ready to use. This will keep for 2–4 days, depending on how cold your fridge is, so this is another one you can definitely make the day before, if wished.

And, of course, if you are cooking for people who are sensitive to spice, you can make this creamy deliciousness without the chipotle.

Almond Butter Satay Sauce

Makes about 250 ml (8½ fl oz/1 cup)

Shopping list
125 ml (4 fl oz/½ cup) almond butter
60 ml (2 fl oz/¼ cup) soy sauce
60 ml (2 fl oz/¼ cup) maple syrup
½ teaspoon tamarind paste, or juice
   of ½ lime
warm water to thin

Place the almond butter, soy sauce, maple syrup and tamarind paste or lime juice into a small bowl and stir until well combined. Add the warm water, 1 tablespoon at a time, until the desired consistency is reached. The amount of water you need will depend on how thick or runny your almond butter is to begin with.

Yoghurt Tahini Sauce

Makes 330 ml (11 fl oz/1⅓ cups)

Shopping list
250 ml (8½ fl oz/1 cup) plain soy yoghurt
3 tablespoons tahini
1 tablespoon date or maple syrup

Place all the ingredients in a small bowl and stir until well combined. Taste. Delicious right? Add a little more syrup if you prefer a sweeter sauce.

Bomb Diggity BBQ Sauce

Makes about 375 ml (12 fl oz/1½ cups)

Shopping list
250 ml (8½ fl oz/1 cup) water
50 g (2 oz/¼ cup) soft brown sugar
2 tablespoons tamari
1 tablespoon apple cider vinegar
1 tablespoon maple syrup
1 tablespoon tomato ketchup
1 teaspoon smoked paprika
1 teaspoon tamarind paste
1 teaspoon Dijon mustard
½ teaspoon sea salt
¼ teaspoon garlic granules

Combine everything in a small saucepan and bring to the boil, lower to a simmer and cook until reduced, about 15–20 minutes, removing from the heat and swirling often to prevent sticking and burning.

Balsamic Reduction

Makes 125-250 ml (4-8½ fl oz/½-1 cup)

Shopping list
500 ml (17 fl oz/2 cups) balsamic vinegar
100 g (3½ oz/½ cup) brown sugar

Combine the vinegar and sugar in a saucepan, bring to the boil, stirring so that the sugar dissolves, then lower to a simmer and cook for about 15 minutes, until the mixture has thickened significantly and coats the back of a spoon. You want to reduce it to about half for a concentrated, but still liquid, concoction and to about a quarter for a thick, glaze-like sauce. Allow to cool, then transfer to an airtight jar until ready to use. It will keep for a few weeks if stored in the refrigerator.

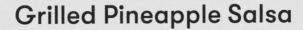

Grilled Pineapple Salsa

*Makes 290-580 g (10¼-1 lb 4½ oz/
1-2 cups) (depending on size of pineapple)*

Shopping list
1 small pineapple, skinned, cored
   and cut into chunks
1 red onion, peeled and halved
30 g (1 oz/1 cup) coriander (cilantro) leaves
juice of 2 limes
2 tablespoons olive oil
pinch of salt

Preheat your grill (broiler) to the hottest setting. Place the pineapples chunks and onion halves under the grill (broiler) and grill (broil) for about 30 minutes, turning regularly, until blackened. Allow to cool.

Place the pineapple and onion in a blender with the rest of the ingredients and purée until smooth.

If using in the next few days, place in an airtight jar and store in the refrigerator.

Walnut Sprinkles

Recipes like this one are often touted as Parmesan, but let's be honest now – it doesn't really taste anything like Parm. That doesn't mean it's not delicious. I love this concoction so much, I could (and often do) eat it straight out of the jar. It has become a household staple for us because, with the Omegas and B vitamins, it's a lot healthier than standard Parmesan – which often isn't even vegetarian – and Louie absolutely loves sprinkling it on his pasta.

Makes about 160 g
(5½ oz/1½ cups)

Shopping list
100 g (3½ oz/1 cup) walnuts,
   roughly chopped
30 g (1 oz/¼ cup) pine nuts
4 heaped tablespoons nutritional
   yeast (about 30 g/1 oz)
1 teaspoon salt
1 teaspoon garlic powder

Lightly toast the walnuts and pine nuts in a dry frying pan (skillet) over a medium heat, then transfer to a plate and allow to cool. Place in a food processor with the nutritional yeast, salt and garlic powder and pulse until the mixture resembles fine breadcrumbs. Store in an airtight jar until ready to use. It will keep for a couple of months.

Magical Mushroom Powder

Dried mushrooms are known for their ability to impart an umami quality to foods and this magical mushroom powder does exactly that. Use it in soups, stews, chillies, scrambles, savoury pancakes, or anywhere you want the flavour of mushrooms without their texture.

Makes 185 g (6½ oz/2½ cups)

Shopping list
60 g (2 oz/2 cups) dried mushrooms
   (I use a combination of shiitake,
   chanterelles and porcini)
125 g (4 oz/½ cup) sea salt

Place the mushrooms and salt in a good-quality food processor, blender or spice grinder. Pulse until you have a fine powder. Store in an airtight jar until ready to use. It will keep for a couple of months.

Corn Tortillas

Makes 18-20 tortillas

225 g (8 oz/2 cups) masa harina
1 teaspoon sea salt
375 ml (12 fl oz/1½ cups) water

I make my own tortillas from scratch, because good corn ones are impossible to find in Berlin, but this is definitely a step you can skip if you live somewhere where they are readily available.

To make your own, you need *masa harina* (flour made from field corn that's been dried, cooked in water with slaked lime, ground, dried again, then powdered into a very fine flour) and water. Having a tortilla press helps too, but it is by no means mandatory - you can also use a rolling pin or wine bottle. They really are the simplest things ever, so long as you don't try making them with straight-up cornflour, which will yield an entirely different result. Each brand of *masa harina* is a little different to the next, but they should have a recipe on the side of the bag.

To make the tortillas, mix the masa harina, salt and water together in a large mixing bowl and knead into a dough. Allow to stand for about 15 minutes, then roll the dough into 18-20 little balls. You will notice that the dough has a unique consistency, almost springy, as if it would bounce back to you if you threw it on the floor (it won't).

Place a dry frying pan (skillet) over a medium-high heat, press or roll a ball of dough out to about 2 mm (¹⁄₁₆ in) thickness, then cook in the hot pan until the edges start to curl up a little, about 1-2 minutes. Flip and cook for another 1-2 minutes, until the edges are lightly browned. Transfer the cooked tortillas to a clean tea towel, stacking one on top of another and folding the towel over to enclose the tortillas so that they steam a little. This is an important final step as the steam will make your tortillas soft. Once all of your dough is cooked, allow to rest in the tea towel for 5-10 minutes and then enjoy immediately, topped with your favourite taco toppings.

Tofu Feta

This recipe was one of my first forays into using tofu. I asked Andy what he wanted for dinner and promised I would veganise anything his heart desired. He asked for a Greek salad, and this this recipe was born. It's since become a staple in our home and I love eating it straight out of the jar, as much as I love popping it on salads and in wraps.

Makes 400 g (14 oz)

Shopping list
zest and juice of 2 lemons
180 ml (6½ fl oz/¾ cup)
    apple cider vinegar
2 tablespoons olive oil
handful of dill, finely chopped
3 garlic cloves, peeled and finely chopped
1 teaspoon sea salt
1 teaspoon dried oregano
400 g (14 oz) tofu, drained
    and pressed

Combine all the ingredients except the tofu in a large jar and stir. Cut the tofu into small cubes (whatever size you like) and place in the marinade. Cover and chill in the refrigerator for at least 2 hours, ideally overnight, or store in an airtight jar until ready to use. Correctly stored, it will keep for up to 1 month. (See photo on page 117.)

Cashew Ricotta

Unlike most other vegan cheese alternatives, this ricotta is made using the traditional ricotta-making technique, but with cashew milk instead of cow's milk. I serve it on pizzas and tacos and stir it through pasta; it's loved by kids and adults alike and no one can believe this is vegan when they try it.

Makes 400 g (14 oz)

Shopping list
120 g (4 oz/1 cup) raw cashews
750 ml (25 fl oz/3 cups) water
1 tablespoon lemon juice

Place the cashews and water in a high-speed blender and blend until smooth. Transfer to a cool saucepan, place over a medium–high heat and bring to the boil. Remove from the heat, add the lemon juice and gently swirl the pan – you don't want to disturb the curds too much. Allow it to stand for 30 minutes before very gently transferring it to a large mixing bowl lined with cheesecloth (muslin) – again, being careful not to disturb the curds.

Rest a wooden spoon across the width of the bowl and tie the corners of the cheesecloth (muslin) over it (see photograph) so that the curds are suspended above the bowl. Make sure that the curds don't touch the bottom of the bowl. Allow to sit for 12–18 hours, pouring out the whey from time to time, to make sure the bottom of the cheese doesn't end up sitting in whey.

If you want to make a double batch, blend the cashews in two separate batches and then combine both batches of cashew milk in the pan. Instead of hanging the curds from a spoon over a bowl (it will be too big), tie the corners of the cheesecloth over a door handle and place the bowl on the floor underneath to catch the drips. Pop a towel underneath the bowl to soak up any splashes.

Transfer to an airtight container where it will keep for about 1 week, if the container is truly airtight. Use as you would any ricotta.

One of my favourite childhood memories is 'baking'. My mum would stand me on a chair at the kitchen bench and fill lots of little cups and bowls with different ingredients. I would 'bake', then she would pop my creation into the oven. Often she would be baking at the same time, and luckily so, as I'm not sure we would have ever wanted to eat what I was creating back then.

My love of baking followed me into my teenage years and as an adult - like my mum - I am often the one to make the birthday and big occasion cakes. Be it for a birth or a break up, me and my cake are always there, either to be enjoyed alone, or as a sweet follow up to a savoury affair.

Although I say preheat the oven at the beginning, you don't necessarily have to do this first. Some people are slow cooks and other people have ovens that get hot very quickly. You know your oven - turn it on when you think is best. People tend to be scared of baking, but I find all of these recipes to be very forgiving, so don't be afraid to play around with different flours, sugars, fruits and nuts, if you feel inspired to do so.

Special Occasion | Sweet Treats

Bounty Cake

A sweet and dense coconut and hazelnut cake, topped with a tangy lemon drizzle and piled high with late summer fruits, this cake is super simple to make and never fails to elicit excited claps and squeals of joy from my loved ones.

Preheat the oven to 180°C (350°F/Gas 4) and line a 26 cm (10 in) springform cake tin with baking paper.

   Combine the lemon zest, sugar, baking powder, bicarbonate of soda and salt in a large mixing bowl. In a separate bowl, combine the vanilla, coconut oil, lemon juice and coconut milk, then whisk into the dry ingredients in the large mixing bowl. Whisk in the flours and desiccated (dried grated) coconut, then pour into the lined cake tin. Bake in the hot oven for 45–50 minutes, or until an inserted skewer comes out clean. Allow to cool in the pan, then transfer to a serving plate.

   Place the icing (confectioner's) sugar in a small mixing bowl. Stir in the lemon juice, 1 teaspoon at a time, until you have a runny icing. Pour the lemon drizzle over the cake, then decorate with berries, figs and hazelnuts, if using.

   This is a very forgiving recipe. If you don't have enough lemon juice, replace what you don't have with coconut milk. If you don't have coconut milk, you can use soy or almond milk in its place. If you don't have hazelnut flour on hand, use almond flour or extra desiccated coconut instead.

Makes a 26 cm (10 in) cake

Shopping list
For the cake:
zest and juice of 2 lemons (about
   2 tablespoons zest and 100 ml
   (3½ fl oz/scant ½ cup) juice)
190 g (6½ oz/¾ cup) raw
   cane sugar
1 teaspoon baking powder
1 teaspoon bicarbonate of soda
   (baking soda)
½ teaspoon salt
1 teaspoon vanilla extract
   or powder
100 ml (3½ fl oz/scant ½ cup)
   coconut oil, melted
250 ml (8½ fl oz/1 cup) coconut
   milk (or any other dairy-free milk)
30 g (1 oz/½ cup) hazelnut flour
200 g (7 oz/1½ cups) plain
   (all-purpose) flour
75 g (2½ oz/1 cup) desiccated
   (dried grated) coconut

To decorate:
150 g (5 oz/1 cup) icing
   (confectioner's) sugar
juice of 1 lemon
500 g (1 lb 2 oz) fresh
   seasonal berries
2–4 figs
handful of roasted hazelnuts

Cardamom & Apple-Rose Cakes

Confused by the method? Don't worry! I popped a video on **www.wholygoodness.com** to show you just how easy these little roses are to make.

Makes 12

Shopping list

6 red apples, cored
vegan margarine for greasing
65 g (2¼ oz/½ cup) spelt flour
65 g (2¼ oz/½ cup) chickpea (gram) flour
pinch of salt
2 cardamom pods, seeds removed and crushed
1 teaspoon bicarbonate of soda (baking soda)
125 g (4 oz/½ cup) apple sauce
125 ml (4 fl oz/½ cup) orange juice
1 teaspoon orange zest
½ teaspoon vanilla extract or powder
4 tablespoons almond butter
4 tablespoons date syrup

To decorate:
icing (confectioner's) sugar

Roses made from apples. This is one of those genius ideas that the internet became obsessed with a few years ago that I just had to try my own hand at. In lieu of the traditional route of rolling the roses into puff pastry, I created a dense and delicious cake base with a sweet and gooey centre to hold these beautiful flowers. The results are mind blowing and these little cakes are complete showstoppers and never fail to impress. The apples roses are surprisingly easy to make but really pack a punch in the presentation department. The oozy sticky centres are a bonus treat that make these a must for any special occasion.

Place a saucepan of water that can fit a steamer basket (or, in my case, a colander) over it onto a high heat and bring to the boil. Cut the apples in half and then, using a mandoline on the number 2 setting, cut the apples into thin slices, placing in the colander/steamer basket as you go. Place the colander/steamer basket over the boiling water, cover with a lid and steam the apple slices for 3 minutes. Remove from heat and set aside.

Preheat the oven to 180°C (350°F/Gas 4) and grease 12-cup muffin tray. Place the spelt flour, chickpea flour, salt, cardamom and bicarbonate of soda in a medium mixing bowl and stir to lightly combine. Add the apple sauce, orange juice, zest and vanilla and stir to combine. Set aside. Whatever you do, don't lick the batter – raw chickpea flour is disgusting.

Combine the almond butter and date syrup in a small mug or mixing bowl and set aside.

To make the apple roses: Place about 10 pieces of apple in a long line, with a generous overlap (I like to place the edge of the second piece in the middle of the first piece and so on). Gently roll up, then curl about 10 more pieces of apple around it, overlapping, until you have a pretty rose. Repeat to make 12 roses.

Spoon 1 scant tablespoon of cake batter into each muffin cup, making a little well in the centre of each as you go. Now, working one by one, spoon 1 teaspoon of the date and almond butter mixture into the wells and immediately top with an apple rose, pushing the rose down firmly when you place it in the batter. Don't spoon all of the almond butter mixture into all the muffins first and then top with the roses, as the butter will run to the edges and you'll miss out on the ooey gooey centre.

Bake the cakes in the hot oven for 15 minutes. Allow to cool in the tray, then remove. You should be able to simply remove them with your fingers, unless some of the date syrup has escaped to the edges, in which case, use a butter knife to loosen the edges. Dust with icing sugar immediately prior to eating.

Chocolate Raspberry Tarts

With the winning combo of raspberries and chocolate, these tarts are perfect for when you need a treat but it's too hot to bake.

Place all the base ingredients in a blender and pulse to combine. If the mixture is not sticking together easily when pressed with your fingers, add up to 1 tablespoon of warm water, a few drops at a time, until the mixture is easy to work with. Divide into 6 balls and press into freeform tart tins or silicone muffin tins (or metal muffin cups lined with cling film (plastic wrap), going up the sides by about 1 cm (½ in).

Place all the filling ingredients in a food processor and purée until smooth. Pour the filling mixture into the tart forms. Top with additional raspberries, melted chocolate and puffed quinoa and place in the refrigerator for a few hours to set. You can enjoy them immediately if you like, they just might be a little floppy.

Makes 6

Shopping list
For the base:
140 g (4½ oz/1 cup) walnuts
6 Medjool dates, at room
   temperature
2 heaped tablespoons
   cocoa powder
pinch of salt

For the filling:
60 g (2 oz/½ cup) cashews
   (soaked overnight or boiled
   for 15 minutes if not using
   a high-speed blender)
150 g (5 oz/1 cup) raspberries
2 tablespoons maple syrup
pinch of bourbon vanilla powder

To decorate:
raspberries
melted dark chocolate
puffed quinoa

Fig & Walnut Crumble Cake

Reminiscent of a baked cheesecake, this is one of my oldest and most loved recipes. If figs aren't in season when you are making this, swap them for berries, as per the OG version of this recipe that you'll find on my blog.

Preheat the oven to 180°C (350°F/Gas 4) and line a 20 cm (8 in) springform cake tin with baking paper.

Prepare the topping by placing the cashews with plenty of water in a small saucepan over a high heat. Bring to the boil, then reduce to a simmer for 15 minutes. Drain, then place the cashews in a high-speed blender with 250 ml (8½ fl oz/1 cup) cold water. Blend until smooth and set aside.

Meanwhile, prepare the cake batter. Combine the dry ingredients in a large bowl with the orange rind, stirring to combine. Pour the orange juice into a measuring cup – you should have approximately 100 ml (3½ fl oz/generous ⅓ cup). Stir in the melted coconut oil, then stir in enough coconut milk to bring the liquid up to 300 ml (10 fl oz/1¼ cup) of liquid in total. Add to the dry mixture, stir to combine and then pour into the lined springform tin.

Cut each of the figs into 8 pieces. Lay the fig pieces on top of the batter mixture, leaving a bit of room between the fruit and the edge of the tin.

Add the sugar, vanilla, lemon juice and psyllium husk to the cashew cream and blend immediately (this is important because the psyllium husk starts to thicken as soon as it becomes wet, and you want it to be evenly distributed through the cashew cream). Pour the cashew cream over the figs, ensuring you scrape out every last little bit of deliciousness with a silicone spatula.

Place in the hot oven and bake for 55 minutes or until an inserted toothpick comes out clean. Allow to cool in pan.

Makes a 20 cm (8 in) cake

Shopping list
For the cake batter:
120 g (4 oz/1 cup) walnuts,
   roughly chopped
270 g (10 oz/2 cups) spelt flour
250 g (9 oz/1¼ cup) raw cane sugar
½ teaspoon bourbon vanilla
   powder
1 teaspoon bicarbonate of soda
   (baking soda)
pinch of salt
grated rind and juice of 1 orange
75 ml (2½ fl oz/⅓ cup) coconut oil,
   melted
approximately 125 ml (4 fl oz/
   ½ cup) coconut milk

For the topping:
120 g (4 oz/1 cup) raw cashews
5 fresh figs, washed
2 tablespoons raw sugar
¼ teaspoon bourbon vanilla powder
juice of 1 lemon
2 tablespoons psyllium husk

Berlin Bliss Balls

In a book that's an ode to my years in Berlin and the connections made with food, I couldn't not include a recipe for bliss balls. The sharing of this recipe sparked the beginning of a beautiful friendship between myself and my dear friend Julia, that began with trips to Berghain and evolved to having babies and going on long holidays together. This basic recipe was shared with me by Julia in 2012 and since then, my bliss-ball making knows no bounds. I often just throw in whatever I have on hand, but this recipe gives you a basic guide to follow. They keep for weeks if stored in the refrigerator (though I doubt they'll last that long), and are easy to transport, making them the perfect sweet treat for picnics and parties alike.

You can use any kind of nut or seed butter in place of the peanut butter. If you have access to dehydrated raspberries, these balls are outrageously good with a few of those added in, or rolled in raspberry powder (which you can make by pounding a few dehydrated raspberries in a mortar and pestle).

Place everything in a food processor and pulse until the dates are chopped and all the ingredients are well combined. Roll into balls and then roll in additional coconut. Store in the refrigerator in an airtight jar.

Makes 10–12 balls

Shopping list
5 Medjool dates
40 g (1½ oz/½ cup) desiccated (dried grated) coconut, plus extra for rolling
2 tablespoons almond flour
2 tablespoons cacao nibs (toasted taste better)
2 tablespoons peanut butter
1 heaped tablespoon cocoa powder
pinch of salt
splash of water

Persian Love Cake

The idea for this cake was given to me by my friend Shan, who is the inspiration behind most of my gluten-free treats. She talked about it for years before I finally got round to making a vegan version for her and, like most recipes that this magical woman inspires, it turned out beautifully the very first time.

Preheat the oven to 180°C (350°F/Gas 4) and line a 26 cm (10 in) springform cake tin with baking paper.

Combine the almonds, coconut, sugar, coconut oil, vanilla and salt in a large mixing bowl and stir to combine – it should be nice and crumbly. Press half the mixture over the base and about 2½ cm (1 in) up the sides of the lined tin. Add the remaining ingredients to the rest of the crumble mixture and stir until well combined. Pour into the prepared base and bake in the hot oven for 30 minutes. Allow to cool in pan.

Serve topped with additional coconut yoghurt, rose petals and pistachios.

Makes a 26 cm (10 in) cake

Shopping list
200 g (7 oz/2 cups) almond flour
120 g (4 oz/1½ cups) desiccated
   (dried grated unsweetened)
   coconut
200 g (7 oz/1 cup) light muscovado
   sugar
120 ml (4 fl oz/½ cup) coconut oil,
   melted
1 teaspoon vanilla powder
   or extract
¾ teaspoon sea salt
3 tablespoons chickpea (gram) flour
2 teaspoons rosewater
120 ml (4 fl oz/½ cup) coconut,
   soy or other plant-based yoghurt
¼ teaspoon freshly grated nutmeg
¼ teaspoon baking powder
additional yoghurt to serve
rose petals and roughly chopped
   pistachios, to serve

Coconut Maple Tiramisu

Serves 8

Shopping list
For the cake base:
400 g (14 oz) tin butter (lima) beans
  or cannellini beans
60 ml (2 fl oz/¼ cup) coconut oil,
  melted
60 ml (2 fl oz/¼ cup) maple syrup
2 teaspoons pure vanilla extract
2 teaspoons apple cider vinegar
½ teaspoon bicarbonate of soda
  (baking soda)
½ teaspoon baking powder
¼ teaspoon sea salt
40 g (1½ oz/⅓ cup) coconut flour

For the coffee liqueur:
100 ml (3½ fl oz/scant ½ cup)
  espresso coffee
4 tablespoons maple syrup
3 tablespoons spiced rum

For the coconut cream:
2 × 400 ml (14 fl oz) tins good
  quality coconut milk, refrigerated
2 tablespoons maple syrup
1 teaspoon pure vanilla extract

To decorate:
1 tablespoon plus 1 teaspoon
  cocoa powder
fresh berries

My spin on an Italian classic, this dessert has been hailed by my loved ones and supper-club guests as even better than the original version. It's gluten-free and vegan, without losing its sweet, boozy, caffeinated richness.

I usually make the cake base the day or morning before I plan to serve the tiramisu, so that it has plenty of time to cool.

Preheat the oven to 180°C (350°F/Gas 4) and line a 28 cm (11 in) springform cake tin with baking paper.

Drain and rinse the beans, place in a food processor and purée for about 30 seconds, scraping down the sides as required. Add the coconut oil and purée for another 30 seconds – it should be thick and creamy. Add the maple syrup, vanilla, apple cider vinegar, bicarbonate of soda (baking soda), baking powder and salt. Purée until smooth, then add the coconut flour while the food processor is still running – it will thicken significantly.

Transfer the cake batter to the lined tin and press flat with wet fingertips. It's an interesting consistency, not like cake batter but almost like cookie dough. Bake in the hot oven for 25 minutes and then allow to cool in the tin.

Meanwhile, make your espresso (or buy it, if you don't make coffee at home). Add the maple syrup and rum, stir to combine, then place in the refrigerator to cool. You want the liqueur to be nice and cold so that it doesn't melt the coconut cream in the next step.

Remove the coconut milk from the refrigerator (the cream solids and water should have separated). Scoop out the cream and place it in a large mixing bowl, along with the maple syrup and vanilla. Using electric hand beaters (NOT an immersion blender) or stand mixer, beat the coconut cream until it's thick and creamy.

To build the tiramisu: Place a tea towel on the bottom of a large lasagne dish or tray and place your serving glasses on top of this. The dish/tray makes for easy transporting in and out of the refrigerator and the tea towel stops them from sliding around. Cut the cake base into 8 pieces, then cut each of these pieces in half horizontally. Place one piece of cake into the bottom of each serving glass. Pour 1 tablespoon of espresso over each, top with 1 generous teaspoon of the coconut cream, then sift 1 tablespoon of cocoa powder over them all. Repeat the cake/espresso/cream layers, finishing with 1 teaspoon of cocoa dusted over the top of all. Arrange berries on top to decorate and place in the fridge.

If you prefer to make one tiramisu instead of 8 individual ones, this recipe works perfectly in a 15 x 20 cm (6 x 8 in) glass dish.

Carrot Layer Cake

Make the icing a day or two ahead, if possible.

Everyone needs a layer-cake recipe in their life, right? And there is no better cake to layer than a deliciously moist, spicy and walnutty carrot cake, stacked and smeared with tangy cashew icing.

This recipe makes two cake layers, but – if you want to pull out all the stops – you can pour the batter into three or four smaller pans to make a taller, skinnier version of this delicious crumb. Shorten the cooking time and use your nose and a skewer to guide you to when they are perfectly baked.

See method overleaf.

For the cake:
500 ml (17 fl oz/2 cups) coconut
    milk or any other plant-based milk
1 tablespoon apple cider vinegar
40 g (1 ½ oz/¼ cup) chia seeds
400 g (14 oz/3 cups) plain
    (all-purpose) flour
380 g (13 oz/1 ½ cups) raw cane
    sugar
2 teaspoons baking powder
2 teaspoons bicarbonate of soda
    (baking soda)
1 heaped tablespoon ground
    ginger
1 heaped tablespoon ground
    cinnamon
1 scant teaspoon ground nutmeg
    (too much can impart a soapy
    taste to your cake)
2 teaspoons bourbon vanilla
    powder
pinch salt
200 ml (7 fl oz/generous ¾ cup)
    coconut oil, melted
540 g (1 lb 3 oz/4 cups) grated
    carrot (about 4 large carrots)
180 g (6 oz/1 ½ cups) walnuts,
    roughly chopped

Serves 8-10

Shopping list
For the icing:
240 g (8 oz/2 cups) raw cashews
120 ml (4 fl oz/½ cup) coconut oil,
    melted
60 ml (2 fl oz/¼ cup) maple syrup
60 ml (2 fl oz/¼ cup) freshly
    squeezed lemon juice
1 tablespoon grated lemon zest
1 teaspoon pure vanilla extract
pinch of salt
60 ml (2 fll oz/¼ cup) coconut
    yoghurt (optional but really
    rounds off the flavour)

For the icing: Soak the cashews overnight in cold water or boil in a small saucepan of water for 15 minutes (don't skip this step). Drain and rinse the cashews, then place in a high-speed blender, along with the other icing ingredients. Process until smooth, scraping down the sides occasionally, until you have a thick, smooth, creamy icing. This will take a bit of work, even in the fanciest of blenders. Transfer to an airtight container and chill in the refrigerator overnight.

For the cake: Preheat the oven to 180°C (350°F/Gas 4) and line 2 x 20-cm (8-in) round cake tins with baking paper.

Combine the coconut milk and apple cider vinegar in a mixing bowl or jug. Add the chia seeds, stir to combine, then set aside to thicken.

Place the flour, sugar, baking powder, bicarbonate of soda (baking soda), spices, vanilla and salt in a separate large mixing bowl and stir to combine.

Add the coconut oil to the chia mixture, which should have thickened by now. Pour the wet ingredients into the dry ingredients and use an electric whisk to combine. Add the carrots and walnuts and continue to whisk the batter until everything is well combined and the carrots have released some of their juices into the batter, making it moist. Pour the batter into the prepared tins and bake for 1 hour or until an inserted skewer comes out clean. Allow to cool in the tins.

To ice: Remove the icing from the refrigerator 1 hour ahead. When the cakes are completely cool, remove from the tins and place the first cake layer on a serving plate. Give the icing a good stir and dollop 3 generous tablespoons of icing onto the top of the first cake layer, spreading it evenly. Carefully place the second cake layer on top. Spoon a little more icing onto the top of the cake and spread this over the top and sides – this is known as the 'crumb coat'. Place the cake in the freezer for 10 minutes (I pop the rest of the icing back in the refrigerator at this point too too if it's a warm day). Remove the cake from freezer and cover with the remaining icing. Top with flowers and pop back in the refrigerator until ready to serve (removing it 30 minutes ahead to come up to room tempertaure). If serving soon, place the cake in a cool spot, out of direct sunlight.

Orange, Almond & Rosemary Cake

Another old favourite, this was originally put in the 'too hard to veganise' basket, until I discovered the wonderful world of aquafaba (see page 9). This recipe calls for a tin of chickpeas, but you only need to use the water from the tin. If you're not turning the chickpeas (garbanzo beans) into hummus or some other yummy treat straight away, you can pop them in an airtight container in the fridge for a few days or the freezer for a few months.

Place the oranges in a medium saucepan, cover with water and bring to the boil. Cook for 15 minutes, drain and then cover with water again and boil for another 15 minutes. After the second boil, rinse the oranges with cold water. This seemingly strange process is what takes the bitterness out of the rind, allowing you to use the ENTIRE fruit in the cake. Roughly chop the oranges, discarding any seeds, and then purée them in a food processor, until no large chunks remain.

Preheat the oven to 180°C (350°F/Gas 4) and line a 20 cm (8 in) springform cake tin with baking paper.

Place the aquafaba and sugar in a large mixing bowl. Using an electric whisk or stand mixer, beat for 3-5 minutes, until the mixture starts to turn white. Add the puréed oranges and beat for another 30 seconds or so, then add the ground almonds, baking powder, vanilla and salt and beat until well combined. Pour the cake batter into the lined springform pan, using a silicone spatula to scrape out all the sweet gooey goodness. Smooth the top of the batter with the spatula - it's ok if it's a little rough. Bake in the hot oven for 1 hour or until an inserted toothpick comes out clean. Allow to cool in the pan.

For the topping: Peel the orange and cut the peel into very thin strips, about 1-2 mm (1/16 in), then juice the orange. Pour the juice into a small saucepan with the strips of orange peel, raw sugar and the leaves from the rosemary sprigs. Place over a medium-high heat, bring to a boil, then turn the heat down to the lowest setting and simmer for about 5 minutes, until all of the sugar is dissolved. Using a toothpick, prick holes in the top of the cake, then gently pour the syrupy topping over the cake. Allow to settle for 30 minutes or so before running a knife around the edge of the cake and gently removing from the springform tin.

Note: If you are wondering what the heck this cake is supposed to look like, you can see a glimpse of it cake on page 5, and also on www.wholygoodness.com where I share a version that's made with clementines.

Makes a 20 cm (8 in) cake

Shopping list
2 oranges, about 500 g (1 lb 2 oz) in total
150 ml (5 fl oz/generous ½ cup) aquafaba (reserved liquid from a drained tin of beans - see page 9)
150 g (5 oz/¾ cup) raw cane sugar
300 g (10½ oz/3 cups) ground almonds
1 teaspoon baking powder
¾ teaspoon pure vanilla extract
pinch of salt

For the topping:
1 orange
60 g (2 oz/¼ cup) raw cane sugar
couple sprigs of rosemary

Chocolate Pudding with Rum Caramel

Serves 8-10

Shopping list:
Chocolate Pudding:
150 g (5 oz/¾ cup) white quinoa
50 g (1¾ oz) dark chocolate,
  roughly chopped
375 ml (12½ fl oz/1½ cups) soy milk
1 teaspoon apple cider vinegar
3 tablespoons chia seeds
115 g (4 oz/½ cup) caster sugar
115 g (4 oz/½ cup) firmly packed
  brown sugar
125 g (4½ oz/1 cup) cocoa powder
1 tablespoon pure vanilla extract
1 teaspoon bicarbonate of soda
  (baking soda)
1 teaspoon baking powder
½ tsp sea salt

Rum Caramel:
1 × 400 ml (13½ fl oz) can full fat
  coconut milk
185 g (3 oz/1 cup) lightly packed
  brown sugar
2 tablespoons dark rum
1 teaspoon pure vanilla extract
½ teaspoon salt

To serve:
Blueberry Poached Pears (page 22)

Nothing says decadence like a chocolate pudding, right?? This one is topped with a rich and boozy rum caramel sauce and poached pears, making it hands down one of my most beloved desserts of all time.

Rinse quinoa in a fine meshed sieve to remove any bitterness, then place in a small saucepan with 375 ml (12½ fl oz/1½ cups) water, cover and bring to a boil. Lower to a simmer and then continue to cook, covered, for 15 minutes. Remove from heat, pop the chopped chocolate into the pot, cover and set aside for another 15 minutes.

Preheat oven to 180°C (350°F/Gas 4) and lightly grease a 20 x 30 cm (8 x 12 in) casserole or lasagna dish with vegan margarine.

Combine soy milk and apple cider vinegar in a bowl and set aside. Add quinoa with (now melted) chocolate and all other pudding ingredients into a blender or food processor. Blend until well incorporated, then while the machine is still running, add the soy milk and puree until smooth. Depending on the power of your machine, you may end up with a lumpy pudding or a smooth one. Both results are fine and outrageously delicious. Once smooth, pour into the greased dish and place in the hot oven for 45 minutes.

While the pudding is cooking, make the rum caramel. Place the coconut milk, brown sugar and rum in a small saucepan. Stir to combine, bring to a boil then lower to a simmer and cook until the pudding has finished cooking. Stir in vanilla and salt and remove from heat.

Once the pudding has finished cooking, let it sit for 10 minutes before spooning into bowls and topping with caramel and fruit. Enjoy, and then go back for seconds, before falling into a joyous food coma.

Note: you can use other seasonal fruit in place of poached pears, however I highly recommend the pears as there is something utterly enchanting about the combination of pears, caramel and chocolate.

Six
Simple Sips

Coming from New Zealand, I'm a die-hard lover of good-quality, crisp, chilled white wine, but a good cocktail also has the ability to hit the spot and make an occasion even more special. My problem with cocktails has always been that they are so expensive to make, because they require so many different spirits and liqueurs. Enter 'Six Simple Sips', a collection of delicious tasting cocktails that won't break the bank!

Cucumber Sake-tini

Straight-up sake is delicious in its own right, but on a hot summer's day I love to make this refreshing drink to go with sushi and dumpling feasts.

Serves 4

Shopping list
½ cucumber, peeled (you can leave whole or roughly chop)
250 ml (8½ fl oz/1 cup) vodka
250 ml (8½ fl oz/1 cup) sake
50 ml (2 fl oz/scant ¼cup) maple syrup or sugar syrup
unpeeled cucumber slices to garnish
lots of ice

Muddle the cucumber in the base of a cocktail shaker. Add the other ingredients, shake with ice and strain into chilled glasses. Top with additional slices of cucumber and enjoy immediately.

Spicy Ginger Margarita

Whenever people tell me they don't like tequila, I tell them they aren't drinking it right. This is my absolute favourite cocktail of all time and I've yet to meet someone who doesn't enjoy it.
Make sure you use ginger beer and not ginger ale - ginger beer is not as sweet but is a lot more spicy.

Serves 4

Shopping list
200 ml (7 fl oz/generous ¾ cup) tequila
400 ml (13 fl oz/1¾ cups) spiced ginger beer
4 limes
1 fresh chilli
lots of ice
fancy salt for rim of glass (optional)

In a large glass pitcher or jug combine the tequila and spiced ginger beer. Cut 2 limes in half and juice them into the pitcher, using your hands to get all the fleshy pulpy bits. Slice the remaining 2 limes into round slices and place in the pitcher. Finely slice the chilli and add to the pitcher. Fill the pitcher to the top with ice cubes and lightly stir to combine (not too vigorously or you will lose the bubbles from the ginger beer).
Rub the end of one of the limes around the rim of your glass and then coat the rim in salt (optional but delicious). Pour the margarita into glasses and enjoy!

Summertime Spritzes

If you're not already aboard the spritz train, it's time to hop on. When I first arrived in Berlin, it was all about the Hugo, but in our last summer there, everywhere I looked there were people sipping on Aperol Spritzes. I've lost count of how many times I've enjoyed them with friends on the balcony of my Berlin apartment on balmy summer nights. Traditionally an aperitivo, I'll gladly take one any time of the night! As you make these cocktails directly in the glass, I've shared these recipes on a ratio basis.

Serves 1

For a Hugo:
ice
sprig of fresh mint
3 parts Prosecco (preferably D.O.P.)
1 part elderflower syrup
splash of soda water
1 lime wedge

Fill your glass with ice. Clap a sprig of mint between your hands and place it in the glass (this will release the minty aromas). Add the Prosecco, elderflower syrup and soda. Squeeze the lime wedge into the glass before dropping it in too. Give everything a jiggle with a spoon to mix it all together and drink.

For an Aperol Spritz:
ice
3 parts Prosecco (preferably D.O.P.)
2 parts Aperol
splash of soda water
1 orange slice

Fill your glass with ice. Add the Prosecco first, then the Aperol and finally the soda (doing it this way prevents the Aperol from sinking to the bottom). Top with a slice of orange. Enjoy!

Deconstructed Espresso Martini

I developed this recipe in my pre-motherhood Berlin days. I wanted to drink an espresso martini but didn't have any coffee liqueur or a cocktail shaker on hand, so I decided to deconstruct things a little. An espresso martini is coffee liqueur, espresso and vodka. Coffee liqueur is espresso, vodka and sugar. So all I needed was the right quantities of espresso, vodka and sugar, right? So right. It worked an absolute treat and was responsible for many hours of dancing in the living room with friends. This is strong, so can definitely be stretched to serve 6 people.

Serves 6

Shopping list
200 ml (7 fl oz/generous ¾ cup) freshly made espresso*
350 ml (11½ fl oz/1½ cups) good-quality vodka
125 ml (4 fl oz/½ cup) maple syrup[†]
ice to serve

Allow your freshly made espresso to completely cool. Pour into a jug or bottle, along with the vodka and maple syrup. Give the mixture a good stir or shake, then pour over ice to serve. Voilà.

Notes:
*We make our espresso in a little stovetop espresso maker. If you don't have espresso-making equipment at home, get some from a café that knows their stuff.
[†]If you don't have maple syrup at home, you can use ordinary sugar – just make sure it's fully dissolved in the warm espresso because you don't want to be sipping on sugar crystals.

Mojito Slushy

This is by no means a unique idea, but it is one that has stayed with me ever since I tried my first mojito slushy at a cute little restaurant named La Cereria in Barcelona, way back in 2012 when we were living in a van and slowly making our way to Berlin. It can be served as a drink or as a dessert.

Serves 4

Shopping list
100 g (3½ oz/½ cup) caster (superfine) sugar
120 ml (4 fl oz/½ cup) water
6 limes, plus extra slices to garnish
10 g (⅓ oz/½ cup) tightly packed mint leaves, plus extra to garnish
120 ml (4 fl oz/½ cup) white rum
6 cups crushed ice

Put the sugar and water in a small saucepan over a low-medium heat. Heat, stirring often, until the sugar is completely dissolved. Remove from the heat and set aside to cool.
Zest 2 limes and juice the rest, so that you have about 120 ml (4 fl oz/½ cup) lime juice.
Place the cooled sugar syrup, water, lime zest, lime juice, mint leaves and rum in a high-speed blender and process until well combined. Add the ice and pulse, then process until well incorporated and slushy. Pour into glasses and garnish with additional lime slices and mint.

Thanks

Andy – for everything; partly for listening to me talk about cookbooks non-stop, but mostly for the mountains of dishes you always washed without complaint, just so I could go and mess up the kitchen again.

Louie – for being so patient with me on our hundreds of supermarket trips and for playing so happily while I cooked our days away. This book wouldn't have been possible if you weren't such an easy baby!

Astrid, Ben, Chris, Eddie, Emilio, Fleur, Hund, Imogen, Josh, Leah, Louie, Maria, Merle, Mikey, Rach, Raph, Sam, Shanay, Shannon and Sophia for being the ultimate dinner party crew.

Alma, Anette, Henry, Iyla, Julia, Junes, Jutta, Tabea, Theo and Phoenix for being the ultimate playdate crew.

Emma, Jessica, Maggie and Sasha – for letting me photograph your hands when lord-knows all you wanted to do was eat the damn food!

Mum – for everything you've taught me in the kitchen.

Kev – for making sure we always ate dinner as a family, and held our cutlery correctly.

Mand – for your scrupulous grammatical eye.

Cecilia Fox for providing me with the best and most beautiful flowers in Melbourne.

Claire, Kajal, Kate and the rest of the Hardie Grant London team for believing in me and making this book more beautiful than I could ever have imagined. Thank you!

About Jessica

Jessica Prescott is the writer, stylist and photographer behind the wildly popular book *Vegan Goodness* and blog *Wholy Goodness*. She grew up in Napier – the fruit bowl of New Zealand – and has spent the last 10+ years traveling and exploring different pockets of the world. In 2012 she moved to Berlin where she wrote this book, and she now lives in Melbourne with her little family who will have a new member not long after this book is published.

Index

Published in 2018 by
Hardie Grant Books, an imprint
of Hardie Grant Publishing

Hardie Grant Books (London)
5th & 6th Floors
52–54 Southwark Street
London SE1 1UN

Hardie Grant Books (Melbourne)
Building 1, 658 Church Street
Richmond, Victoria 3121

hardiegrantbooks.com

British Library Cataloguing-in-
Publication Data. A catalogue
record for this book is available
from the British Library.

Vegan Goodness: Feasts
by Jessica Prescott

ISBN: 978-1-78488-166-5

Publisher: Kate Pollard
Commissioning Editor:
Kajal Mistry
Senior Editor: Molly Ahuja
Publishing Assistant: Eila Purvis
Art Direction/Design:
Claire Warner Studio
Photographer and food styling:
Jessica Prescott
Editor: Emily Preece-Morrison
Proofreader: Lisa Pendreigh
Indexer: Cathy Heath

Colour Reproduction by p2d
Printed and bound in China
by Leo Paper Group